A LATE DATE

A LATE DATE

FINDING LOVE IN CYBERSPACE

ANNE THURSTON

TATE PUBLISHING
AND ENTERPRISES, LLC

Published by Tate Publishing & Enterprises, LLC
127 E. Trade Center Terrace | Mustang, Oklahoma 73064 USA
1.888.361.9473 | www.tatepublishing.com

Tate Publishing is committed to excellence in the publishing industry. The company reflects the philosophy established by the founders, based on Psalm 68:11,
"The Lord gave the word and great was the company of those who published it."

Published in the United States of America

ISBN: 978-1-68319-082-0
Family & Relationships / Dating
16.05.03

My Thanks Yous

Every person in my life has enriched it.

My family; for love, understanding and outreach

All of the amazing men I met on my dating journey. For each of your unexpected help, experiences and information: Ron, Clayton, Vaughn, Dusty, Ken, Bill and all the rest I met online.

Nannette Dion for her perfect advice

Michele Cortright for her special help

Grace Otte for her love

Pastor Paul for his understanding

Melissa Kelsley for her outreach

Ray's daughters for their lesson

Don Clemer for his outreach

Phil Dickerson for his advice

Chris for his foresight

Susie and Pat for their open door

Laura, Rachael and Pat for their arms about me

Debbie Phillips for her special words

Paul Pellett for being the man he is and his love

David Thurston, my son who has made my research possible from start to completion.

David Leo Cook for always being with my writing

Paul Pellett's family for their reception

Jim Cook, Jason Letterman and Roger Herman for being my computer teachers

Joyce Maynard., Mardi Link and CD Brennam who shared writing skills they had learned during their careers.

Boyne Writer's Circle and all their suggestions

In memory

Edward Asher Thurston

1920 – 2009

Ww11 Air Force vet, d beloved husband and father

The Difference

Solitude is the delicious moment of aloneness
When one's entire being dwells outside itself
In an awareness of complete wholeness
Nothing more is desired

Loneliness is the numbness of half a human
When the other half has vanished, deserted
Not to be returned until life on earth ends
It is not meant to be

Contents

Prologue

Telling my story of online dating is going to take a while. What I have to tell the world is going to be hard for it to believe. But I don't lie. I'm ninety-two.

I discovered long ago lies bring trouble to everyone. I feel it is important others understand why my story came about. Why I did what no one else I know would have even considered getting involved in.

I went online to find a man. Yes, a man to continue living a meaningful life of love. For sixty-five years, I had lived with my wonderful Ed. His life he shared with me filled every moment of mine from our first date during WWII back in the 1940s until his last with me in 2009.

When I opened online's door, I had no knowledge as to where I would travel, or suspect over four hundred men would hold out their hand to me. They all shared my dream because they too had lived long lives wrapped in love. To live without it was unthinkable to each.

Most were in their homes desperately wanting to travel, laugh, and share all that was theirs with someone. Their lives had been beyond their expectations—there was a retired supreme court judge living on a Florida farm, Oregon US medical researcher, Pennsylvania college professor, Indiana author, WWII deep sea diver, San Francisco manufacturer, Wisconsin four-hundred-acre dairy farmer, a retired North Carolina minister and doctor of Psychiatry, Pacific oil driller, and almost anything else in today's world.

They had lived their lives with beloved wives and children. They had made mistakes and experienced the unexpected just as I had.

In fact, it was all because of the way my life differed from others I know that I sit here today.

I believe it happened the moment Ed, my husband, and I began our second life. Yes, when he was seventy and I sixty-eight, we started ours all over. Our widowed daughter died of cancer at thirty-nine and left us her three wonderful children back in '91. I remember her last words to me so well as I stood beside her hospital bed, holding her hand: "Mom, would you and Dad take my kids and parent them after I am gone?"

Once again, we became a mother and father. The time was different from the earlier days of our own four children. Ed had retired and was home to help me care for the little six-, eight-, and ten-year-old grandchildren. It was a together project. His work at the Port of Toledo had prevented him from being with his own children day after day.

The first day of school for them began five days after their mother's funeral. I turned to Ed as we watched them climb aboard their school bus and giving him a hug, said, "Can you believe us? We're back in our thirties again. It is another beginning in life for us. What are you thinking of?"

He tightened our hug and in his deep voice, told me, "Oh, my Snorky, I am thinking down the road. We are going to travel whenever we can. We are going to do for and with these little treasures all we couldn't do with our first family. You and I are going to live a second life."

And so it was. He and I became active as members of the band boosters, painting scenery for dramas and attending one special event after another. I ended up on the school board and became instrumental in obtaining new school buildings complete with electronics for our little town.

This gift of being given such an unexpected and unbelievable life to live rapidly dissolved our deep grief over the death of our Mary as well as that of her brother, Tom, who had also died of cancer the year before.

It gave Ed and me a second life. No one else we knew ever had such an opportunity to remain young and active. Those our age simply went into retirement and played bridge or golf. Others felt sorry for us seeing it as nothing but a burden of work. They were completely wrong.

With the grandchildren, we returned to downhill skiing in our seventies. Before church in the morning, Ed would pack the car with all our ski equipment while I packed a picnic lunch to have in front of the large fireplace in the ski resort's homey lounge. The area was just north of Petoskey on the side of one of its hills. Once Ed parked the car, he would throw open its tailgate and call out, "Come get your gear. Gram has your lunches. Just follow us into the lodge, and as soon as you have eaten, we'll get out on the slopes."

We traveled, camped, and studied the history of our great country. I remember when Ed, who during WWII had served at the air force's headquarters in Washington DC, decided to take the children there for a week's exploration. The five of us actually fit into a Pullman bedroom with all its hideaways. The grandkids had a ball with all its gadgets, pullouts, and push-aways.

This was the summer following their arrival with us. We had just completed a new two-bedroom and bath addition for them on the northern end of our out-in-the-country home. It was on the edge of a steep hillside, so it allowed us to build their two bedrooms as a split level.

Ed turned to me and suggested, "Let's stick Pat on the top floor and the girls in the lower level. They'll each be just a half flight to their bathroom."

Within a year of their arrival, Ed installed Alba's old post office window in the wall of the girl's closet. We had bought it at an auction sale down in Elmira. Originally used in an area's grocery store, it had individual postal boxes in its surface. Each could be opened on the hall side with a key. The mail was inserted from its backside. Ed placed this all so the lock side faced the little landing halfway down the new stairs. The open side faced into the girl's closet. The three had a ball playing post office hour after hour. They set it all up so each had their time as the "postman" in the closet.

When summer arrived and we headed out for Washington, Ed unloaded the four of us from the train in Washington, DC, handing each of the children a little inexpensive camera to enjoy recording the days ahead. He instructed them, "See the little button on the top? All you do is hold the camera up to your eye, find what it is you want a picture of, and press the button. The picture will be yours forever."

He was such an exceptional man. The five days we were in our capital city allowed Ed to share with his grandchildren all he had learned during his six months assignment at the air force's headquarters in Washington during his army days. With their precious cameras, each left with pictures of those things and places which caught their interest and eyes. They learned the value of photography.

Today I have thousands of snapshots tucked away in books, boxes, and folders of places I have been and things I have done. Not a one did I take. Looking at them brings back the memories of the three grandchildren clustered around their grandfather and saying, "Oh, look at this one I took of the old airplane." It had been on exhibit in Washington.

The oldest, Laura, who is now thirty-four, utilizes her photography to create illustrations for the cooking articles, "Prairie Flavors," she now writes monthly for Oklahoma's rural electric company's magazine, *Oklahoma Living*.

Ed was with the children as their father until the day he died. By then, Laura and Rachael had completed college; Pat was still attending. Today, although off in their own wonderful lives, they are still my children via e-mail, car, or plane. This is very special as in addition to our son Tom and his sister Mary, the grandchildren's mother, I have also lost my other daughter, Nancy. She left just two years ago at sixty as the result of an almost unknown heart problem. David is the only one of our four children still here on earth with me. He is so special to me over and over again.

The experience of becoming a mother a second time gave me the opportunity to understand life simply doesn't end because of age. No, I can move forward as long as I reach out to find something which needs my love and attention. So here I am telling my story.

1

Why Me?

Give me another few minutes before I plow ahead about my great adventure in cyberspace. Much as I want to dive right in and tell my online dating story, I feel the need to share some other things about myself and why I set forth into today's unknown world of cyberspace to find another life.

The process of aging today creates a final understanding of ourselves. It's all about where we've been, we've known, what we've done, and how it all has made us the person we are.

Because of my grandfather, mother, father, brother, and husband, I am very different from many women. Yes, there was only my brother, David, and myself. We were close in age. There were no sisters. He was a year and a half younger than me.

Grandfather was ninety-four when his life ended. We were special to each other as he had had throat cancer surgery and could not talk, just make sounds through a small hole in his throat. He taught me to lip read. His hugs and hand holding walks through his orchard to look for mushrooms were a highlight of my preschool days

Father was an architect-contractor. Because he was a speculative builder of upscale homes, we were constantly on the move. At no time prior to my college years did I live in one home long enough to make friends. David and I became each other's best friends. It bound us together our entire lives although we ended living very different ones.

My mother tried to make a very feminine gal out of me, but I resisted piano after six years and dance lessons. She became a nationally known floral arranger, and I even backed off from that. No, I was all wrapped up with learning how to draw house plans with my father and working in his vegetable garden per his instructions.

On his annual September Canadian trips, he took us all to fish from canoes. I was in his, David in Mother's. There on the lakes of Canada, I became part of our world's outdoors. The trees on the distance shorelines, the fluffy white clouds in the blue sky overhead, and the music of the water's touch on our canoe all filled me with such a love of the outdoors it remains my treasure to this day.

My husband, Ed, took me a number of times up to the Canadian Soo to board its big east-to-west train. We'd climb into a passenger coach, not a tourist one after stacking his canoe in the baggage car. Our backpacks went onboard with us. The train clutched us and headed westward, well past the tourist attraction waterfalls, almost to Wawa.

It was then Ed would pull the rope next to his seat saying, "Well, Snork, here we are. Let's climb off and get on our way."

The train would come to a stop way out in nowhere. With the conductor's help, the canoe would be unloaded, and the train would be on its way. There in the midst of nowhere, both of us with our backpacks full of gear headed out into the Canadian wilderness, the canoe in Ed's arms.

The two of us would penetrate the forest, using lakes and rivers to move away from the known world into our very own of water, sky, and trees with its birds and animals. We would hum our happiness as we penetrated the wilderness.

I had become an avid athlete thanks to my brother, David. I even paced him over hurdles (Father made a set for our big yard) as he prepared to be a track team member.

I never dated in high school. I didn't look at boys as anything other than friends and athletes. Beside all this, I was 5'9" tall. Most of the fellows were shorter. I was 100 percent a tomboy! *Sex* was an unknown word back then. There weren't even kisses allowed in the movies.

Like most women, I knew nothing whatsoever about the world of men which lay ahead of my life's path. My mother never shared a bit of it with me. Even during my high school years seeing her enema bag dangling from a hook next to their toilet didn't tell me a thing other than she had bowel problems I imagined.

And of course, my father wasn't supposed to mention a word about it all either. Nor did my brother, although I am certain being on his way to manhood, he understood it all clearly.

By the time I reached my senior year in Burnham High School in Sylvania, Ohio, I was its class vice president, had written its school newspaper, been part of its radio program, competed at the state level in algebra, was the girl's baseball team's catcher, a basketball guard (we couldn't leave our net end of the court as it would have been too much activity for a girl), and in its drama productions. Because of my height, I was always the play's old lady. Never was I the beautiful, romantic star on the stage.

As the year approached its end, both graduation ceremonies and the senior prom were about to happen. It was a great surprise when the Dean of Women (and drama coach) halted me in the hall between classes one day and said, "Anne, please bring your prom date to my office with you tomorrow during the activities hour after lunch. I want to give you your instructions pertaining to leading your classmates out onto the dance floor at the prom."

This appalled me. I had no such date. I had no plans to attend the dance. I didn't dance. I blurted out, "Oh. I can't. I am not attending the prom. I have no date."

"But, Anne, as your class's vice president, it is your duty to help the president lead the parade out onto the dance floor. Get yourself a date and be at my office tomorrow. With that, she turned her back and began to walk away.

I called out to her, "Okay. I'll be there. I will ask my father to be my date."

She stopped dead in her tracks. Turning, she asked, "Your father?"

"Yes," I responded and turned to be on my way.

When I reached home, I discovered the dean had called my mother. Mom was waiting. She immediately told me she thought my father would not enjoy going to the dance. "Can't you think of someone to take you? How about Buck?

I shook my head. Buck was one of my best friends at high school. He was also a graduating senior, but not anyone I wanted to dance with. Then my mind suddenly remembered Jimmy Corey, my across-the-street neighbor and playmate back in the days of the Great Depression. We had been fifth graders together.

We had had wonderful time. One day, he and I had picked violets in our hillside woods next to the Maumee River to tie into bunches and sell from a roadside table we set in place. Some guy in a black convertible stopped and bought all five bunches for twenty-five cents. We were so excited!

Turning back to Mother, I asked, "What if I asked Jimmy? Would you call his mother and see if he could come over? I know we would have fun."

Mother looked completely confused. Having kept in contact with Mrs. Corey, she ended up shaking her head "Okay" and made the call. Jimmy's answer was a yes. He'd get over by driving his father's car. Back in those days of '41, no teenager owned a car. He was living in Cleveland about a hundred miles to the east. I didn't realize I was doing something unheard of in those days.

When he arrived and parked the car in our drive, I about lost it all when he climbed out. He wasn't the Jimmy I remembered in the fifth grade. No, he was a tall eighteen-year-old young man of unbelievable handsome looks! I have often wondered what he thought of me, standing there in my yard waiting—all 69 inches of me!

There was no "Hello" hug. That wasn't done back then. Rather he grinned my way and called out, "Are we picking violets?" We both laughed and never stopped all evening remembering the time we had been together.

We had a wonderful time. I learned to dance quickly, and we never ran out of something to talk about. My classmates were speechless when they saw me in his arms! That summer, we had a couple of dates, and he even showed up down on the OSU campus to see me in the fall.

I remember the date in Cleveland at his fraternity's fall party. One of the acts each new member was to perform was to kiss his date beneath a flower-decorated archway. Jimmy explained it all to me and asked, "Is this okay with you?" I assured him it was. After all, he was a good friend I thought a lot of. And that was that.

At Ohio State, my goal was to become a doctor. My parents didn't buy the idea. According to society, the profession was only for men, not women. Dad sat me down and suggested, "Anne, you have such exceptional ability in the world of art. The works you have done the last four years at your Toledo Art Museum studies are unbelievable. I hope you will continue studying it down at Ohio State. Let the men be the doctors and you add your art to the world. Think about this seriously, please. Your mother and I love you so. We want you to be happy."

Although Dad had left OSU his freshman year to enter the WW1 air force, my mother, who lived there in town, attended the university and obtained her degree in nutrition back in 1915. This was all but unheard of in those days. She ran the food service for a large Red Cross TB hospital in Southern Carolina during the war. I remember her address book from those days—filled from front to back with the addresses of service men—privates through generals.

2

Locked Doors

The very first week I was on the Ohio State campus studying art, I met the man who would become mine. Like almost every other major happening in my long life, I had nothing to do with any of it.

No, it was entirely my mother's work. The second day, I was on campus and in my room getting settled and ready to start classes two days later when a call came into my room from the front desk. I had a phone call waiting for me. I hustled out into the hallway, picked up the receiver, and said, "Hello." It was Mother. Instead of asking me how things were going and about my train trip, she started right out, "Anne, I happened to talk to Ruth Thurston yesterday."

Ruth was a woman my mother's age who attended the same church in Maumee. Mother kept right on talking, "Her son, the middle one, Ed, is a senior down there at Ohio State. We think the two of you should meet, so Ruth is asking Ed to take you out on a date. You remember him, don't you?"

There I stood in my dorm's hallway miles from home and my mother was telling me to go on a date with some old guy—he was a senior there on campus. I couldn't believe it!

"Mother, no way. He is an old guy, and I don't date and don't want to. No way, Mother."

"Now, Anne, think this over. The Thurstons are friends of ours. Their sons are fine young men. You are there alone, and it will be nice to have a friend. Go on this date with him, please. If you

23

don't want to date any more, that will be your decision. Have a good time. I have to hang up now—my three minutes are up. Bye."

I heard the line go dead. The three-minute long distance call term had expired. My father wouldn't permit extending service time. He felt the extra charge it added was too expensive. The date would happen. I was furious and scared at the thought.

Sure enough, in the evening, Ed called and confirmed the date. "Anne? This is Ed Thurston. Mom tells me you are down here on campus. I'd love to say hello. How about a Coke tomorrow evening? I'll pick you up at seven. Okay?"

He sounded okay, but that didn't relax me a bit. I had no idea what I was supposed to do when he arrived at the dorm to walk me down the street to a Coke bar in a drugstore. His age and status of being a university senior were just too much for me to handle. I struggled with what to wear all the next day.

My first glimpse of Ed as he arrived to stand at the base of the broad, curving stairway leading down to the front dorm parlor, remains in my mind. He was tall and handsome. His smile and sparkling eyes sent an overwhelming message throughout my body. Nothing like that feeling had penetrated me during my times with other guys, even on my dates with Jimmy.

I remember thinking on the spot, "There's the man I am going to marry." Ed's and my love only grew. We shared one experience after another for sixty-eight years; sixty-five of them with him as my husband until he left me in death in '09.

My entire life has been wrapped up in the man's world. Unlike society would have me believe, I have learned men are not to be leery of, fight with, or ignore. The Lord created them the way He desired. Then He gave them to us so our lives could be as great as possible.

Yep, I am an old woman. Old enough to have my family think the best place for me following my husband's death was a local retirement center. This all began as my husband of sixty-five years approached his death on January 2009 with Alzheimer's. I'm sure they meant well. It was what families all over the country were doing with old and lonely widows. My small town of only 3,500 residents had been home to me over fifty years. It had four different choices to offer its women.

I remember so well my son, David, saying when he called one day, "Mom, have you thought of looking around there where you are and finding yourself a nice place to retire into after Dad leaves? That big new one up on Division Street looks as if it would be great. If you want my help, just give me a call. I'm here for you."

I knew he was there for me. He always had been. He was the duplicate of his dad. But I was healthy! I loved driving my car, getting around town whenever I pleased, where ever I wanted, for whatever reason I could cook up. It made me feel alive. I had no desire to sit back and watch myself evaporate into space or heaven, whichever you endorse.

I strongly embraced the promise of heaven. I was raised, as was common back in those early years of the 1900s, to endorse the Christian faith. Back then, most mothers were not career orientated but stayed home doing household chores without today's electrical gadgets. I can even remember helping my mother with the laundry in our basement. She had two large metal tubs and a sink plus a hand cranked wringer.

Without any synthetic fabrics in existence, there were days of hand ironing to be done after the laundry dried hanging outdoors on a clothesline and then was sprinkled with water.

Each day of the week had specific chores to do. Monday was laundry, Tuesday, ironing, Wednesday, sewing, and mending, and so on until Sunday, which was a "no work time." It was then David and I attended Sunday school and my mother ingrained my thinking to embrace the Bible's world. Ed and I did the same with our children. He even sang in the choir for years, and I taught Sunday school over fifty. Today's generation is not gathering in the same attitude about Sundays and their lives. It concerns me as it has been so important to me.

I am sitting here remembering those times as Ed approached his death and shaking my head in disbelief. I am so glad I thumbed my nose (behind their backs, of course!) at my family and did what my heart yearned to do; find another man to love. My sixty-five-year marriage to Ed had been wonderful from start to finish.

It was because of the happiness and togetherness the two of us shared year after year I understood what a relationship between a man and a woman could offer. I believed I had to have someone to share my life with. Together we would have a dreamlike end of life.

After all, Ed and I had shaken our hands long before his last days promising each other to go on living once one of us left. Only then could he leave me without worries. I was to find another. As he held my hand, he pulled me into his arms, "Snorky, remember this promise."

I murmured, "You too, Big Boy."

Our handshake didn't happen out of the blue. No, it was my wonderful mother's advice she gave me.

In 1983, eighteen years before Ed was diagnosed with Alzheimer's, Mother died suddenly from a case of flue. She was eighty-four, living by herself in the apartment she and my dad were enjoying upon his death four years earlier. We all assumed she was her usual happy self. As it turned out, we were way off on this assumption.

I drove three hundred miles south to spend a long weekend with her to celebrate her birthday that year. There were nearby people we knew and visited as well as Toledo's unbelievably large and great art museum. My brother, David, and I had studied art there during our four high school years. He came by a few times to visit with me at Mother's. I remember his saying, "Sis, remember the time you helped me extract a tooth in the woman who I discovered had cancer of the jaw?"

I answered, "Oh, Doc, every time you called me in to help you when one of your nurses wasn't able to get to work something went on I still remember. How about the man who sat there in your dental chair and flirted with me while you did his root canal?"

The day I had to leave Mother's to head back home was a beautiful sunny late April day. We hauled all my stuff down the stairs to the back door and out to shove it in the car. When I backed out of it and turned to say good-bye, I discovered Mother with her arms outstretched for a good-bye hug. At least I assumed it was.

But, no, she grabbed me, all 5'4" of her. Holding tight she told me, in a firm, clear voice, "Anne, don't ever believe it when someone tells you, even a minister, that your life will return to happiness in due time after your husband dies. This is not true. During these past four years, I have missed your father more with each passing day. Every morning I pray the day will allow me to die and join Trace in heaven. Remember this and share it with Ed."

It was then we enveloped ourselves in our good-bye hugs, and I drove off. The tears slowly slid down my cheeks as I headed north to my Ed.

Of all the dire predictions my family and friends shared in their effort to keep me off-line, the one I will never forget was my brother, Doc's. Only a year and a half younger than me, we shared our entire years.

During the early years, we bonded so deeply I grew to understand men in a way many women are never given the opportunity to. At the same time, I am constantly shaking my head over the way women live, often not at their choice.

At that point in time, Doc had had five wives. I guess he saw himself as our family's relationship expert. Because of this, I called to tell him about my dating plans, "Doc, I suspect my plans to go online to find a man is going to knock you over."

He laughed out loud. He was a dental surgeon. He was just plain laughing at me. And he didn't stop laughing; just kept it up long and hard until I edged in a question.

"What do you think of my idea?"

"Sis, you don't know men."

"How can you think that? Ed and I were married sixty-five years?"

"Sis, do you know research claims a woman thinks of sex just a couple of times a month, but men think of it every seven seconds, even guys in their eighties?"

Again the laughter; Doc was eighty-five.

"I suspect you read that in some girlie magazine. How in the heck could anyone research such a subject? Don't people know by now women lie? If the report said every seven minutes instead of seconds, I might consider believing it. But there is no man alive who can have a separate thought motivate through his cranium and change it to yet another subject in only seven seconds, let alone one about sex. Give me a break!" I refuted.

More laughter; then in a choking voice, "Go ahead, Sis. Do your research. But if you're going to date, think about getting a small revolver."

"Not to worry, little brother," I said. "I'll have my knitting with me. I use size 13 needles."

"You won't get them on a plane, Sis."

"Guns, either, Buddy!"

I could tell he was ready for our conversation to end, but before it did, he made me promise to keep him updated.

"I promise," I said. "Absolutely, on a daily basis."

He was still laughing when the phone went dead.

Doc's laughter was good-spirited. He accepted both me and what I was about to do. It gave me courage.

Remembering his words, I said to myself, "Get yourself going." After Ed's passing, I announced to my family and friends I was going online to search.

About this same time, I had a phone call from my oldest son, David. Yes, we named him after my brother. He lives a hundred miles north of me in Michigan's Upper Peninsula with his Cathy, a fantastic gardener. After his father's death, he considered me his responsibility.

After our "Hellos," he said, "Mom, I know you never locked our home and strongly suspect you don't your apartment either. But now that Dad is no longer with you and everybody in Boyne knows you are alone, I think you should always lock your door. Not just when you go out but even when you are there alone. That way no one can enter your place unless you want them to. Okay?"

I understood his thinking. Most others would think the same about any old woman living alone. I promised him I would although the whole stupid thing ticked me off.

In our small town, few people locked their doors. The whole idea made me feel like a prisoner; locked away from the world. But I kept my promise.

3

639 Miles

I admit this adventure of mine made me shake my head, laugh, and even cause a tear to drop now and then as it unwound.

The very first day as I opened my computer online site, I sat and shook my head at the men who were looking at me. They had all knocked on my door. Despite the dire predictions from my brother, once I announced my plan to invade cyberspace and join online programs, they arrived seemingly no different from any others my life had known. They didn't look at all dangerous or scary.

Yes, I went ahead despite all the warnings tossed my way to look for another man. I had promised my Ed I would. For all those years he had held my hand and walked me through the woods of Canada, on board ocean liners, and even down ski hills, I had remained unharmed. My life had been wonderful even though absolutely nothing like I had ever been led to expect.

The only other place to look for a man was a bar. And women my generation knew what they'd find. When you think about it back in our youth, we looked at bar rooms exactly the way online ventures are seen today. For we women, they were a big no-no. So there I was online, sitting for my first day in front of my computer, today's no-no.

Among the men I saw in front of me, one sat quietly smiling into my eyes. I realized immediately there was absolutely no way he could devastate me. After all, I had been with men every single one of my years. Before I married Ed, my father was my favorite to do things with. I was not some uneducated teenager. I was an old woman.

Even today with a smile on my face and hilarity within, I remember Mr. NYC, and think of him, or "Hessitant99," as he called himself. There he was, a charming, dignified man with beautiful wavy black hair and a fascinating profile.

His letter proceeded to deepen my excitement. I half disbelieved such a man would be the first to reach me in cyberspace.

> Dear Helen,
>
> I have read your profile and have come to believe we should pursue a conversation with the goal of getting to know each other better. Perhaps we will form a friendship that will lead on to other things.
>
> I am a retired US international financier, having served a Wall Street firm as well as its overseas offices. Besides English, I speak French and Italian.
>
> I live in the UES Manhattan. You will read of my activities in my profile. I find that we share many similar interests.
>
> I look forward to your reply.
>
> Harvey

I had been in a high school French class for two years. All but a couple of the words had long since deserted my brain. I never had the opportunity to be in France long enough to use its language. He mentioned he lived in the UES, which meant nothing to me.

I replied.

> Dear Harvey,
>
> Your photo intrigues me; the great eyes and better yet, smile. What is the saying? "A picture is worth a thousand words"?
>
> I can't imagine life in a huge city. Couldn't we settle on a mutually desirable area and both visit it when we are in

the mood? Or does that strike you as too much of a leap into your future?

Almost everything you are seeking is very present in me. It would take considerable talking to explore my potential and to understand where I have been so far.

Your work sounds very interesting, and I assume would take considerably more hours to share. There's where our problem lies. At our age, time has taken on such a new dimension; not to be taken loosely and certainly not squandered.

Please check out my online info and take a look at my eyes and smile.

At this point, I stopped and gave online dating some more thought. If I was going to play the game of pen pal with lonesome men, I figured I'd best follow the rules and insert a photograph of myself. I hadn't managed to persuade myself to fiddle around to do so at that point. But having experienced my reaction to Hesitant99's photo, I knew I had to.

I recalled a snapshot my son-in-law, Paul, had taken about two months before when my first story, *The Book of Anne*, was published. The only bad thing about it was I was sitting in a rocking chair—an old lady chair. I wasn't keen about the photo, but it was the only one I had to use.

I cropped it down to just my smiling face. Before completing my letter to Harvey, I figured out how to insert the photo into my profile. It gave me a sense of accomplishment. "Hey, I can do this computer stuff!"

I returned to writing my letter.

I think you will be pleased. And note what I am searching for. I am serious (although laughing at myself for even getting involved in all this), but loneliness and boredom have done this to me—about who it is I want to live with the rest of my life. That you might be the one seems a possibility. But there are a few others also.

Take a look at my age. Although I consider it a man-contrived subject, having zero to do with the person to which it is affixed. I certainly do not look or act my age. My health is unbelievable. It's my Irish genes as are my humor and brains. Heck, my smiling eyes and good looks are all thanks to the Irish and their blarney.

The one thing I can see as a minus for me is that I am not wealthy. You didn't divulge an annual income figure either. But remember, two plus two still adds up to four. And if one is a great mathematician, two and two can equal more. With that to think about, I am signing off. You'll find more about me on my website: *www.23thurston.com*—don't try the blog as it is under construction.

I hope to hear from you,

Anne (my name is not Helen Cook—she was my mother). One question: What does UES mean?

Perhaps the greatest advantage to online dating, especially for older people, is the speed at which connections are sometimes made. It wasn't the next week, but that very same evening, I had Hesitant99's reply.

Dear Anne,

Your letter is so complete that the least I can do is answer pronto! I am flattered that a lovely and intelligent lady like you would consider me a potential match or friend or lover—whatever!

There are however 639 reasons against our even trying to find a common path. UES means Upper East Side (of Manhattan)—a desirable address.

In many a way our respective profiles would make it logical we at least try. At least my pragmatism strongly advises me to the contrary.

Thank you for writing, Anne, I really appreciated your message and am glad to note that there are others. Good luck and kindest personal regards.

Yours truly,
Harvey

His answer was so obviously about UES and 639 it rather ticked me I hadn't seen it immediately. He must have thought me not too bright. How embarrassing. He was referring to the number of miles between us. My reply reminded him Cleveland was a wonderful meeting place and only a little over three hundred miles for each of us.

In his answering letter, he remained the gentleman who had knocked on my door wishing me wonderful success as I continued my search. He was certain some fortunate man would be thrilled with such a beautiful gal! I responded in a very ladylike answer, praising him for what he was doing and wishing him success. I said I hoped we could remain occasional friends online.

But that was not to be. The very next moment, I learned the hard way about one of the digital services available to online correspondents. A certain button can be clicked to slam the door in the other's face, refusing to accept any further correspondence from them. This notice arrived on my screen in large black type: HESSITANT...HAS BLOCKED YOU FROM FURTHER COMMUNICATIONS WITH HIM.

Talk about speed! I'd been approached, met, and dumped within thirteen hours! I was ticked off such an educated man, one who had worked his entire life with the public, would stoop so low as to slam his door in my face. It was a good thing for him 639 miles separated us.

I refused to let one bad experience turn me away from online dating.

4

Thumbing My Nose

It was bedtime. I tried to sleep. My mind spun back and forth over Mr. UES. Not as a person but rather the things he'd just taught me.

A complete novice, I had been unbelievably fortunate to have him knock on my door. Like many Midwesterners, I hold certain awe about New York City. The huge number of residents and their extreme differences—the museums, stages, and arenas as well as the news media, both spoken and written—caused me to shake my head in disbelief. I reminded myself everything and everyplace in this huge land I called mine were unalike. This included me.

I had been to New York City five different times to National Needlework Wholesale Exhibits with my P's and Q's quilting pattern business back in the 1980s. With our oldest daughter, Mary, as my assistant, I visited its stores, theaters, and restaurants, and listened to the unending city noises rising above its narrow streets. I remember them keeping me awake at night in my hotel room nine floors up in the air. Ambulances and fire trucks both were emerging upward. Every person I sat next to or passed on its sidewalks was a stranger. They were all city folk.

Mary agreed with me New York was a different world than ours in Michigan.

As we worked our booth in the huge shows, we would look out across the crowd of visitors and then at each other and shake our heads in amazement. Turning to me she'd whisper, "We live in America, Mom. Every person out there is different from the rest of us."

"And tonight I know a New Yorker," I said to myself as I looked at my computer twenty-five years later. "Well, not actually know, but corresponded with him. I don't even have any idea what his name might be." As I snuggled in bed, I tried different ones. Yet somehow none fit.

He'll remain Harvey to me for all my days. Or "Mr. EUS." So much about him had been shared in so little time. He disproved everything all my friends and family had tried to warn me about. I knew his kind. They were managers of established professions and businesses who greet in a warm and interested manner as they listen to your reason for being seated in their office.

They were in their suits, crisp shirts, and subtly beautiful neckties; polite and kind, they endeavor to be of help. I could envision Harvey before his bank retirement. Oh, yes, I understood who he was. He was not a dangerous stranger.

And he recognized himself and his needs; as a pragmatic man who was certain of himself because of his pragmatism. However, there had been a twinkle in his eyes as he wrote me. He was a man who was intense, steady, yet ready to roll up his sleeves to hold what he desired. I perceived a possible seven-second man of Doc's.

I prayed he would find the woman who would fulfill his desires and who, in turn, would know she had found the man of her dreams. Because he was my first, I understood for certain I could never forget him. He managed to make me feel right at home in cyberspace. I was more determined than ever to reach my goal—a man to love.

Yes, his abrupt departure had angered me; having had no idea about the "door closure" the online services offer their subscribers. Now I did. Thank you, Harvey, for all you have taught me. It is amazing.

And because of my suspicion about his age, I had to admit to myself I was severely handicapped in the area. Society equates age with mentality, health, and mobility. All three are treasures supposedly belonging only to those younger than we octogenarians, yet we overflow with them ourselves and those with whom we live.

I was certain my age, as close as it was to ninety, would make my search next to impossible. Yet even a 5 percent possibility was better than giving up. I was certain there were men out in cyberspace who were even over their ninety-year mark, lonesome and ready for a piece of yummy apple pie.

At least this was what I believed. My brother's take on all of this, as being only a result of male seven-second thinking simply didn't fit the picture.

As for Harvey, I would have the last laugh. By being there and knocking on my door, he strengthened my resolve to regain the happy, love-filled life, which had left me when my beloved Ed died in late January. My age wouldn't matter even though most others will view it with caution. I needed loving.

Smiling, I locked my apartment door for the night. The world of cyberspace I had just stepped into had no doors and therefore no keys. It was limitless, so I no longer felt imprisoned when my door was firmly locked as my son had requested.

The sun was shining in my window when my eyes opened the next morning. As I stretched and felt myself coming alive, I heard myself saying, "Oh, hello, Harvey. Hope your day is sunny, and you are feeling great. I am."

Chuckling to myself, I rolled into my lifetime morning rigmarole but with far more speed than I had for some time. I was anxious to open the computer and see who might have knocked. If no one had, I planned to take my first plunge and knock on some guy's door myself. After Harvey, I admitted I had absolutely no idea where I was headed yet was excited about the possibilities.

Sure enough, I had five knocks and the system I used the day before displayed six new possible choices for me to approach. This last was a real temptation. I decided to do my own knocking even before opening my day's mail.

Before me on the screen were six profile photographs. All were of men in their eighties and from the far corners of the USA. They intrigued me. I found Georgia, Florida, California, Kentucky, Texas, and Pennsylvania. There was a retired college professor, a US Supreme Court judge, a lawyer, an owner of a trucking line, an editor, and a Texan.

Their listings of favorite pastimes and places all varied as well as their choices in music, food, reads, and sports. Each, in his way, seemed interesting.

As I studied my choices, I never once stopped and said to myself, "Anne, do you have any idea where this search is going to lead you? Or who you are going to meet? Or when?" No, I was too fascinated in what was there, right in front of me, on my computer in the little town of Boyne City off in the forested area of Michigan.

Tucked between the great lakes Michigan and Erie, I wasn't thinking of California huddled by the Pacific or Malaysia, tucked on its surface. Nor did my mind wander off to Florida, New York, or Maine and the Atlantic.

I didn't look at my kitchen clock to check the time. It was of no importance to me. Subconsciously I had convinced myself although my search might not happen within a few days that it would end around the corner in the near future.

It never entered my brain the number of men I would get to know a little or a lot would be over four hundred. Heavens no! Nor could I have composed a list of lifetime occupations I would rub elbows with. Nor the places, families, happenings, honors, adventures, rewards, achievements, and such I would learn about.

A book reader all my life due to the Maumee library directly across the street from my home in Maumee when I was a preschooler, I always had a book within my reach. My shyness kept me where I knew who it was standing near me. Within books, there were never strangers for me to hide from. The stories made my world extensive. I was so content.

It was easy for me to decide to send off my own short "knock on their door" letters. Basically the invitations to correspond I sent out were the same but each with small changes to better fit the profile I was considering. The first went on its way to a retired college professor at the University of Georgia.

After seven notes to him, he proved to be a UES and slammed my door in my face. Each in its own way proved fun to do. A man in Pennsylvania in a town on a little river which he loved to fish in stayed with me with e-mails for weeks. We so enjoyed hearing from each other.

Another just two hundred miles south of me in Michigan never let himself consider me as "next door." No, the millage was like a towering wall he could never climb. We had both been on Guam. He served at the same air base Ed did and on which I lived during Ed's time during the Korean War. Our times didn't overlap, but our memories of the island surely did. His memories of the island's sudden rain showers which left those beneath the sky soaked echoed mine.

Unfortunately as we wrote, he developed an intense and invasive eye problem. Last I heard from him his five daughters were at his side helping him adjust to his new life. It made me sad to realize if he had reached out to me, the two of us could be together—his life could have been so much more meaningful. Just the thought brings tears to my eyes. He had taken eleven midwinter excursions by boat in the Atlantic. He could have continued doing so with me along. There were other men with similar decisions to make.

In the midst of all this, I received an invitation to correspond from Texas. Talk about miles between. There was no comparison with those between me and the man south of me in Michigan.

My being online was so crazy! The mileage wall made no sense. He wrote,

> Anne,
>
> You look and sound delightful. I wish I didn't live a half a world away (in Austin, Texas).
>
> Bill

Attached was a photo of himself seated on a brown horse. A navy-blue cap was pulled way down over his eyes. Guess the sun was bright down in that part of our world.

> Dear Bill,
>
> I don't know whether you would be interested in me. My age could be a factor, although it shouldn't be—people I meet think I am in my late sixties or early seventies. My goal in taking part in this e-mail search is twofold. I want a great man to live this part of my life with and I want to give that man a wonderful companion for the rest of his. Please check out my photo and site. It is posted under Norkie.
>
> I am willing to relocate—but would love to summer up here in God's world.
>
> Anne

Despite the miles, he estimated them to be somewhere around 1,500. Our contacts continued every day as I roamed about the country meeting one man after another. Bill and I truly bonded.

5

Twelve Hours

The next "Hello" was to the Scotsman. He proved to be unbelievable and will never be forgotten. I suspect he will remain in many minds.

I asked, "Why are you at sixty-four endeavoring to open a friendship online with a woman twenty-five years older than you are?" His answer proved interesting.

> Helen,
>
> Thanks for getting in touch with me and very much fine hearing from you and knowing you from this site. I want you to read my message carefully and answer all my questions. Let me start by telling you a little about myself. My full name is Jack McLaughlin…what about yours? How long have you been on this site? I joined a few weeks ago. I haven't got time to get on it. What do you think of the site? Do you believe in Internet dating? Though I never believed in Internet dating, I have some testimonies from people who had made success through it. Have you seen anyone that was lucky to meet his/her soul mate through Internet dating? Haw many guys have you met or communicated through Internet dating? How was your conversation with them? Do you still keep in touch with them? I wish you could tell me what you think of Internet dating. What is your height and weight? I am 5'11" tall. What is your occupation? What happened to your past relationship? What kind of relationship do you

really wish to have? What have you learned from your past relationship? What kind of relationship do you really wish to have? Do you think a relationship can work out between us due to the distance? Have you ever traveled out of the country? What is your religion, favorite color, date of birth? I am a Christian, blue is my favorite color, I am born on 26th May 1947. I work as a contractor with the well-known oil company AGIP Scotland Oil Company as a Contractor. Do you live alone? What are your favorite activities? Your favorite music? Your favorite color? What do you do for fun? From my past relationships, I have learned to be careful, think twice before getting into a relationship. I believe someone must have to study a woman's physical manner and approaches before getting into deep relationship with her. I want someone caring, honest, and lovely to share my life with. I need a very serious relationship because there are lots of women out here for games. I want to know your mind. I believe honesty, faithfulness, and open-minded are the foundation for a good relationship. Feel free to ask anything you want to know about me. I am a simple and very open-minded man. Don't be afraid that I will get upset if you ask any questions. I look forward to your reply. Have a nice day.

Jack McLaughlin

I wrote him the very next day, answering all his twenty-three questions. It took me five whole pages. His long letter was without paragraphs and some of his word choices seemed strange. It made me wonder if English was his language. I didn't find any of them invasive; perhaps because they were just things I wanted to know about him.

I did ask again about our age difference.

Anne,

Age has nothing to do with who we are or what we are. At sixty-four, I am no longer a youth. I have had a life, which has been full of both disappointments and joy. I am certain this is true for you. Why shouldn't we seek friendship? I find you lovely and very interesting.

Jack

He then proceeded to tell me he lived on the edge of Washington, DC, on the Atlantic Ocean. He expressed his deep love for the water and how he spent hours watching it come ashore. He owned a deep-sea oil rig, which he operated for a Scotland company. He had lost his entire family in a car accident a few years before and lived alone, missing them.

He was certainly not a New York City banker or a silent Georgia professor. His disregard of my age was a challenge to me because of my interest in writing online. And so our letters began. Back and forth they flew; each becoming increasingly friendlier and sexually suggestive at his end. Despite our age difference, I began to suspect Doc's seven second theory. The same was true of the daily letters Will and I were exchanging.

The next morning, I received a dozen roses, embellished friendship cards, and even a Christian poem from Jack.

The unbelievable occurred about five days into this adventure with the Scotsman at 4:00 a.m. Sound asleep in my big, comfy queen-sized bed; I woke up as the telephone rang outside my door on a little hallstand.

Unaware of the time, I still knew it was during the night because my window was black with stars. As quickly as I could, I untangled the covers and made it to the floor feet first. Then I was out the door grabbing the phone.

Since we had moved to Boyne City, there'd been two other times I'd been awakened by a phone call in the wee morning hours. One was the night our son-in-law, Patrick, died at thirty-five in his bed at 2:30 a.m. Another was a drunk who'd called a wrong number to request a ride home. So when the phone rang, I didn't think it was an emergency, but I was prepared for another drunk.

"Hello," I said, rather briskly, "who is calling?"

The answer was immediate, but the voice had such a thick accent I couldn't make out a single word. Then, I heard "Scotsman."

"Scotsman?" I said. "Where are you? What time is it?"

"Oh, my darling. What time is it there?"

The words sounded blurred. In my half sleep, they sounded as if it was a real Scotsman talking. Oh, I thought, so the caller is not an American. I didn't think any further. I was still too groggy.

After turning on the hall light and looking over at my clock, I answered, "Four o'clock. Why, what time is it where you are?"

In the same heavy brogue, he answered, "Four p.m. I am in Malaysia, halfway around the world from you. I am so sorry, my darling. I will call you tomorrow afternoon."

When I first went online all those months ago, I never dreamed I'd be getting phone calls in the middle of the night from halfway around the world!

Oh, yes, I thought, the Scotsman is an oil driller. How I remember crossing the timeline out there in the Pacific Ocean on my trip with our little children back in 1952, to be with Ed on Guam during the Korean War.

Ed had become discouraged in his effort to become a painting contractor, which my father had suggested on his return from WWII. Behind my back and I was pregnant with our Mary, he reentered the air force. For five unbearably long months, Ed and I were separated as the air force endeavored to place him on their Guam air base. He was in San Francisco when our Mary was born.

It was New Year's Eve in 1954 when I found myself with our two sons, two and four and Mary, six weeks huddled in a Chicago hotel bedroom waiting to board a train the following day.

I remember the hotel porter the next morning as he endeavored to pick up my large suitcase. "What do you have in here? A piano?

I answered, "No, canned formula for my baby. They don't have that brand on the island I am traveling to."

After a week in barracks in San Francisco waiting for our ship (there were twenty mothers and families), we were told to be ready to board the ship. It was at the dock. I was the exception. The captain sent me word; my children and I could not make the trip; Mary was too young. She had to be six months old, not six weeks.

Ed had warned me of this as due to his intense loneliness for all of us, he had changed Mary's birthday in his records. I was to handle her as if she were older. I had tried to do so. Suddenly I learned my act hadn't worked.

One of the women I had come to know came up to me and said, "Anne, give us Mary. We will see to it no one knows where she is and you can join us on board." To this day, I have no idea how they managed it all, but my children and I all made it to Guam. Mary was returned to me after the ship left San Francisco.

Once on board the ship in San Francisco, all of us except Tom became desperately seasick. Our trip was the roughest the head man had ever experienced. My three-year-old son had "sea legs." He walked on a slant!

My arrival and the feeling of Ed's arms as they wrapped themselves about me have never left. Even the flat tire on his car when we were ready to head down the island to our home did not prevent us from an intense night of "Hellos"!

And there I was, fifty-four years later, talking to a man who was working on an island in exactly the same dateline. Small world! Crazy world!

By then, I was wide awake. Our chatting and laughing continued for a half hour or more.

About a week later, Nancy, my second daughter and the Presbytery minister in Lake City, came up for a visit to work with me on a book she was writing. I was to illustrate it. I loved doing it together. I was also working on illustrations for Tom's wife, Sue Ellen.

She had rewritten a book about the moose on Isle Royal Tom had written the summer he had graduated from Houghton University. She had turned his story into a wonderful poetry form for young children. Again, since Ed and I had hiked the Island three times, I was having a great experience doing its illustrations.

Nancy was a graduate of Central Michigan College, where she had set out to become a grade school teacher as her sister Mary had. Somehow the teacher who oversaw her practice teaching weeks prior to graduation so discouraged her she changed course and entered the University of Dubuque Theological Seminary in Iowa. It was a wise choice, although time after time, she would experience a congregational member who felt all ministers should be male and made it difficult for her.

Our work was spread out on my small dining room table and we had our sleeves rolled up, deep into our project, her children's book titled *The Colors of God*. With such a title, you can imagine the fun I was having with my paints. The phone rang.

The voice was so loud it reached Nancy's ears; I saw her look up. With my hand over the speaker, I told her, "The man from Malaysia." She rolled her eyes and shook her head violently. "No, Mother, no!"

His voice was loud with exciting news. He was traveling somewhere, but I couldn't figure out where. His distortion of American words was unbelievable. In desperation, he spelled for me. "M-I-C-H-I-G-A-N."

"Michigan?" I asked in disbelief.

Yes, Michigan. He was planning to come see me, traveling halfway around the world to be with me.

I promised I would send him some recommendations as to where to land, etc. There were choices south and north of me.

I finally hung up and turned to Nancy. She was shaking her head no vigorously. Laughingly I assured her I had things under control, explaining to her, "This isn't about me but about a special man who will enrich my online adventure. I need to know why my old age is being ignored. Do you have an explanation?"

She shook her head no.

So it was I sat down and wrote about Mackinac Island and Traverse City as possible locations for him to secure his air travel. I reminded him the Internet would show him all kinds of information about each area.

I would drive to meet him at the airport he chose to take him to his hotel. I was certain he would want some time to rest before we headed out to spend time together. I assured him I would have a room for myself in the same hotel.

His response came the next day. He was sorry, but his e-mail service was not functioning very well and he said he would have to get back to me later. His words brought no disappointment or surprise to me. I had suspected this fascinating man was suffering from a rather acute case of "seven minute" syndrome, way off on the other side of the world. To be involving me with his affliction was surprising, to say the least.

Was the world that different in faraway lands? Are American men finding themselves willing to solve their problem with an ancient old bag like me? It was beyond my imagination.

But then I had never lived in another land; never been away from the USA for any length of time. I had traveled with Ed many times, but we never lingered except for the one year on Guam. And I wasn't alone like the Scotsman; I had Ed and three of our children with me.

A month later, having heard no further from Scotsman, I wrote him a short note urging him to continue his search, but advising him to stay within his age group.

His tart reply arrived soon after.

49

"I don't need your apology. I have been so honest to you, and all you could say is to hurt my feelings after all my effort on trying to make this work 'cause I really want you in my life. I want you to know that you have ruined everything without us even meeting in person...As for me, I will remain single again till I die. Not even thinking of dating any one again. Bye for now!"

Not even a signature. I remember I felt terrible this had to end as it did, but I saw no other answer. I still believe I did the right thing. I feel certain he eventually returned to online dating. He was so good at it.

6

Fishing

There I was, a woman who had outlived her husband and two of her children intent on keeping the promise I had made to my Ed back in 1984.

I never dreamed in years back I would become so ancient. But then, why would I have foreseen the way changes in our foods and of our life would affect my generation's longevity? Oh, yes, and those younger than me, people yet to come. They will all become possible centurions.

All life stories are full of laughter and tears. That's the way this world of ours moves. The impossible, improbable, and unexpected are always right outside our doors. Remember the moment love arrived? When feelings exploded throughout body and mind? Yet it was only with physical contact our understanding and realities fell into place. I was eighteen when this part of me came to life. I remember my first glimpse of Ed standing at the foot of my Ohio State University dormitory's stairway

That was 1941. World War II was on. The next spring, Ed graduated finding himself in the air force. Yes, I dated an "old man," a senior, all during my freshman college year. We attended every sporting event, including the swimming team's splashes. We never missed a campus dance.

The huge library became our hang out as I landed the job of caring for the upper floor's restricted collections. A large desk near its balcony's edge would be spread with our homework assignments every evening.

Ed loved to dance. He was always asking, "There's a dance on campus yet this week. Will you go with me, Snorky?" Dancing back then was very personal, nothing like today's. I was held within Ed's arms. Snuggled against his body, I could feel every muscle move as he swept me over the dance floor. My head could be tucked tightly against his and the rhythm of the music would file our bodies.

One time at a dance held in his dormitory, I remember his close hold and becoming aware of something tucked down in the front of his trousers. All I could conclude was that he was carrying a flashlight with him for some reason. Why it wasn't in his side pocket made no sense to me. Eventually I figured that one out!

At the end of the college year in '42 and a couple of weeks before he left to be in the service, we attended the senior prom. Held in the heart of Columbus at its huge hotel, the name of which my sloppy memory fails to remember. We made it there in my Uncle Ralph's Cadillac.

He lived out in Bexley on the eastern edge of Columbus and surprised Ed by calling him on the phone and asking, "I hear you and Anne are going to the prom next week. Would you like to use my car?" The city's largest insurance salesman, he had the money for such a vehicle, a beautiful large Cadillac.

Ed was so tickled. He wore his tux with tails, different from most of the men who stuck with the plain version.

On the other side of the story is the formal I wore. Having none, I set about to make a beauty. In my search for a suitable fabric, I ran into material costs way above my ability to handle. It was then I discovered some thin white fabric in the curtain department for much less than any of the rest.

I bought the necessary yardage, returned to my dorm room, and proceeded to cut out and hand sew my fantastic swishy gown. Once sewn, I decorated its entire bottom edge with lovely, embroidered red roses. Ed was impressed.

We loved the orchestra and danced every single number they played. I can still hear Ed whispering in my ear as it nestled against his face, "I love to dance with you. You are so tall and beautiful. I am the luckiest man on this floor."

We married the following year. After Ed's graduation and Washington, DC, assignment, he became the transportation officer at Camp Pinedale in Fresno, California. Our honeymoon was an overnight trip on board a cross-country train returning him to his work.

However, the honeymoon began the night before in Toledo's big hotel, the Perry Davis. We made it downtown from my parent's home about eleven in the evening after all my aunts, uncles, and cousins had left the reception Mother and Dad had held at their home. I have never forgotten that night.

Most of my clothes had been packed for our journey out to California in a huge trunk, which Ed had stashed into the back of his father's car he was using while at home. His parents lived in nearby Maumee where I had spent my grade school years.

For the hotel, I had stuffed my things into a small bag I could handle myself. In it was an outfit Gladys Grover, a close friend of Mother's had hand sewn. I remember Mother saying, "Anne, you are so fortunate to have such a beautiful outfit for your honeymoon. Gladys just has her two boys, no daughters. She has always envied me for having you. I am certain her love for you is behind the things she has sewn."

And they were special. Made of shiny silver-white satin, there was a petticoat, bra, panties, a nightie and its robe. Beautiful lace trimmed it all. The pieces fit me like a second layer of skin. I had worn the underwear beneath my wedding dress—of course, no one could see it. But I was looking forward to standing before my Ed in the gown. I could just hear his words of appreciation.

Once in the hotel room, Ed said to me, "Go ahead and use the bathroom to get ready for bed. I will undress out here."

So I took off and quickly attired myself in my gorgeous white satin nightie. Its thin shoulder straps held the floor length gown as if it was only another layer of my skin. Being five foot nine and weighing only 130 pounds, I hoped to take Ed's breath away.

When I opened the door to the bedroom, I found him standing by the bed stark naked. I couldn't believe my eyes! But what he called out was what I will never forget.

"What you have that on for? Get it off and get over here. I want you in bed with me." And I had thought he would view me as beautiful! What a blow.

It was that night I learned what it is men do with their wives. About two weeks later, out in Fresno, California, Ed set the rule for our marriage.

"Honey, I am going to have to back off making love to you every night. From now on, I will every other night."

And so it was. No matter how I might plead, it was never any more frequent until prostrate surgery just before our fiftieth anniversary made intercourse impossible for him. Our last fifteen years were void of it, yet our love simply continued to flourish and grow. I was fortunate without knowing it as Ed was prolific in "tuning my fiddle."

Once settled into an old brick apartment, I became a Fresno State College junior. None of this part of my life was anything I could have imagined as possible. Women seldom find the life they dream of. Back then, it was very much a man's world. I believe it still is despite the radical changes women have fought for during my lifetime.

Even though my intent when I left home in 1941 was to earn a degree as a medical doctor, it was never a real possibility. No, the world had other things for me to do, see, and recognize.

My life has been in good hands—those of another. How can I say such a thing? Because of the life I have experienced. It belonged to me only because it was given to me so I could help others find theirs.

My hope is that as life-length expectations increase, others will view such a gift as something they can share with another. Not allowing a slammed "online door" cause discouragement. It didn't me. No, if anything, it just made me more certain I would stick with the whole setup and find the man I hungered so for.

We war wives back in the 1940s weren't "in" the war officially. Yet our lives were yanked and jerked about day by day because of it. I was one of the lucky ones. Ed had the foresight to enroll in OSU's ROTC classes, which awarded him the position of an army officer.

By the end of my sophomore year at OSU, Ed had received the position of transportation officer at Camp Pinedale, a large base in central California just north of Fresno. It proved the perfect answer for me to continue college at Fresno State.

None of this was my decision. It was just what life handed me. I doubt if I ever thought about my plans to be part of the medical profession back in those topsy-turvy times. It was all about my husband, who he had become, and the world in which he found himself. To me, it was an adventure woven into my life because of the man I so dearly loved. I so admired him.

After his death, I knew I had to get on my computer and find another man. Hessitant99 and Mr. Malaysia didn't discourage me. Rather they made me understand I must continue to contact many other men to find "the one."

7

Seven Seconds

Will and I were online chatting together for most the time I was with Malaysia. It helped me make the decision I did about Mr. Malaysia.

Another was Smacker. One look and I knew I had found a possible man I might find interesting and enjoyable to know. There he stood; leaning against a large tree trunk. The inscrutable smile, the keen eyes, and the casual attire screamed academia. I found it difficult to believe what I saw. What was a man like that doing online hunting for a woman? It just didn't make sense to me. Reading his profile only added to my disbelief.

Smacker was a college professor. In fact, he had worked himself up the ranks of his career to have become a writer and lecturer as well as a teacher in his field. Although perhaps trivial to some, his 6'2" really attracted me.

My eyes returned to the classic navy jacket with its brass buttons and the open collared shirt and the broad shoulders, and I heard myself say, 'Oh, yes!"

I set my fingers immediately on the keyboard. He never responded to me.

We remember the happenings within our lives from different angles. I learn this over and over when listening to others recall an event which left them shaking their head, laughing themselves silly or unable to move, so terrified. Sitting here and letting my mind wander back five years I admit what is there, tucked in my mind is simply unbelievable.

How did I so confidentially and positively set forth into cyberspace? How had I convinced myself it was the right thing to do? Was it Ed's words and his firm hand clasp? Ed and I never discussed "how" I would locate another man. Back in those days, no such opportunity as online dating knowingly existed. No, the how just slowly penetrated my world as I watched my love, month after month leave me. It was obvious to me our handshake was absolutely all he required to die in the peace of thinking of me as one who would continue her life with another.

Unlike so many others who leave our world because of Alzheimer's, Ed's personality never changed. There was no development of belligerence, swearing, abuse, or abnormal behavior. No, to the very last moment we shared, he remained the wonderful Ed I had always had. He knew me and even his immediate family when they came to see him. He slowly backed away from carrying on a conversation yet he was cooperative with me and the hospice women who came a couple times a week to check his vitals and give him a bath.

From the very first bath, they knew not to go down below his waist line. He had raised his hand in protest the first time the nurse endeavored to do so. Not a word was said. It wasn't needed. There he lay on his back in "his" hospital bed, an army officer.

Nancy had hung large-framed photos of his grandchildren and great-grandchildren on the walls around the room. I believe her doing so gave Ed the impression he was home even though we had moved him out of our home up on the hillside into an in town apartment.

The hospice women caught on immediately. I laughed as it was his army air force behavior. He was very serious and was to be obeyed. They got the message. I became his "below the waist" bather.

His mind left him slowly in other ways. I became aware of it in his reading. All our years together, books had been his pastime. Even when TV entered our world, Ed had no interest in it at all.

He continued to read magazines, books, and newspaper to gather all the information he sought.

Eventually I obtained a wheelchair I could stash in the car when I headed north to Petoskey with Ed to watch baseball games.

"I love this field," he said the first time. "Of all the fields I've played on, this is the only one on the shores of a lake. It's a good thing these men can't swat the ball hard enough to send it swimming."

In the fall of '08 during the race for presidency in our country, he had begun in the early summer to follow the candidates closely. Slowly, his reading degenerated to just the headlines and that eventually left. No newspaper or book was picked up. He simply could not remember just what he had read in the preceding line. He never uttered a word of complaint. In the earlier days when he was seated in our old overstuffed chair, he merely laid his head back, closed his eyes, and drifted off to sleep.

It was all but impossible for me to believe Ed had no reaction to President Obama's victory—our first black man to gain this country's top office, and Ed was completely unaware of it.

At the end, hospice gave me a special medication to slip under his tongue to ease his breathing problems. The second night I did so, I sat on the edge of my bed, which was close to his. Holding his hand in mine, I whispered to him, "I love you so much, my darling." His hand squeezed mine in response. He was answering, "And I love you with all my heart, my love."

Then I silently prayed, "Please, dear Lord, take my Ed as he sleeps tonight. His life has been so wonderful he deserves its end, not another hour of this way too long trip."

Ed left me by morning. I had been so fortunate. Not once had he run away from me or made my life difficult. No, his love was mine all the way.

8

Foundations

The first part of my online adventure had been simple. It took no great thought or work to gather together the equipment I would want by my side as I stared at my computer. After all, we had raised our three grandchildren, and despite the beautiful yet expensive set of encyclopedias I bought for them to use, they introduced the world of computers into our home. Not once were the encyclopedias opened.

No, I had entered the world of online equipment way before most of those I knew my age. I even purchased a desk chair with wheels. I foresaw hours online and felt I deserved a comfortable seat to live in. The pillowed back against which I could lay back and think has been great.

My years of living as a woman in a man's world were in a state. Seated in my new chair, organized and ready to take off, I decided to do a little research. The reaction I had had from close friends and family when I announced my plans had been so negative and weird it made me wonder where and how they were coming up with it all.

My wonderful and lifelong friend, Grace, had shaken her head firmly and sternly told me to back off from my plans. "You're just asking for big trouble, Anne. And you know my advice about your driving. You are about ninety, and that means your driving days should be over. You know my car is no longer parked downstairs waiting for me."

There I stood in her comfy apartment in down town Boyne City. Its broad window doors allowed her to look out across her balcony onto Lake Charlevoix's long stretch toward Lake Michigan. She stood before me in her darling dress looking at me so sternly.

Yes, I knew. And I felt she was making a big mistake. She was so well and full of get and go even if a year older than me. But I didn't argue. I loved my car and the way it expanded my life. Fortunately, there was no city nearby. My driving had nothing to do with heavy traffic. Basically it was through small towns and the beautiful countryside. Boyne only had two traffic lights and probably a hundred stop signs.

Back in the '40s, I had struggled so to learn the how of driving. Of course, I went to my father when I was sixteen and asked, "Dad, can you find the time to show me how to drive?"

He was out in the garage, bent over looking for his saw when I found him.

Standing up, he looked at me and said, "I've been waiting for you to hit me with that question. Now would be a good time. Here we are in the garage next to the car. Come on over here and let me show you."

With that, he strode over to the car's front and popped up the hood. There it all was. All that stuff which made the big REO go down the road. He always bought REOs as he felt as a contractor he should appear successful.

Looking my way, he pointed to one of the gadgets under the hood. "This is the starter. It—"

I interrupted, "No, Dad, I don't give a hoot about all those things. I just want to sit behind the wheel and start the car up, back it out of here and be on my way."

"Anne, the way you do something is to understand what it is and why it does it. Now, listen to me."

Utterly disgusted and impatient, I turned my back and strode out of the garage across our home's big lawn with its mown grass, huge elm trees, and Mother's flowers and headed in to my bedroom.

I knew exactly what he wanted to do in teaching me how to drive. He had pulled the same thing on me back when I was almost six. I had managed to climb up on the high stool before his big oak drawing board one day when he was off at work. I pulled up a piece of paper and grabbed one of Dad's sharp pencils and began work on a house design. I had watched him do it so often.

Suddenly I heard his voice, "Anne, what are you doing on my board?"

I dropped the pencil expecting to be yanked down to the floor. "I'm drawing a house."

Without touching me, he leaned over the board and pulled out another sheet of paper. "Now watch what I do," he explained to me.

"When I draw a line on my paper, you draw the same line on yours."

He began with the footers, explaining they held everything in place once the house was built. From there, he worked us up to the floor joists, studding, stairs, windows, doors, ceiling, the second floor and then the attic, roof, chimney, and shingles. We both had "designed" a cross section of a house.

Down through the years, I have designed many houses or their remodeling. But the most important thing is Dad taught me whenever I approached something I knew nothing about I should begin at its base and figure out how to achieve whatever it was I wanted to have or find.

This has led me into all kinds of projects I otherwise would have decided someone else had better take care of. The most exciting took place the day after Ed moved us all up to Boyne City in '61. Late that afternoon, I gathered the four kids and walked them over to the library about two blocks away from our wonderful big old home. It had been built back in the lumbering days by one of the area lumber masters.

The library was of the same era. It was brick, a large dignified building—a Carnegie gift to the little town. We climbed up the stairs to its large front entry and then on up to its large front room where the librarian stood behind her desk.

I explained to her, "These are my children. We just moved in to town yesterday, and I'd like to get all of us library cards. We just live over on Lake Street."

She was old and didn't smile or greet us. No, she had a frown on her face as she replied, "I can give you cards today, but they won't be worth anything in a month. All our books have been given to the new high school's library. It will be opening then. We will close."

I couldn't believe my ears. "I don't understand. How can a Carnegie library lose its books and be closed? What will the people in town do?"

She just shook her head and proceeded to make out our five cards. The kids immediately ran over to their section to find what they wanted to take home with them. What the librarian had said meant nothing to them.

At home after dinner, I shared this all with Ed. "It's bad enough, darling, to live in a town where no one talks to you and we know no one. But not to have a library makes it impossible. I am going to call the state library and see what can be done."

"Sounds like the thing to do," he replied. "And, Snorkie, don't get upset with the people here. They all believe your brother fired the ski hill manager for no good reason. They aren't happy I am replacing him. Just let it go. Don't argue with them. As they get to know us, they will change their minds."

So I was off, starting with the footers. The state board explained the step-by-step procedures to follow starting with the city commissioners and on to the state's delivery of an all new five hundred new book collection and the opening of the library's door. A woman, Janet Waldner, I didn't know heard what I was up to and joined me.

Thanks to Janet, the city commissioners offered their support with a small annual tax benefit, and she became its main librarian until her retirement year arrived. Back about ten years, a woman of the area left a large sum to the library, which doubled its size and permitted the installation of computers for its members.

In the days, weeks, and months which followed the no-luck driving lesson, neither Dad nor I brought the subject up again. So it was on the day I married I still hadn't learned to drive. Ed didn't seem to think it was important either. After all, he drove and I was his wife.

The following year, an officer's wife I met at "on-base functions" one evening asked me, "Anne, you don't drive, do you?"

I nodded my head in agreement.

"Well, how about it if I teach you. Would you like that?"

Her concerned look reminded me the desire to drive was very alive in me. Without hesitation, I replied, "Oh, what a great offer, Debbie. But where and how?"

So it was the very next day after my classes she arrived with our car which she had picked up from Ed on base. Holding the door open on the passenger side, she leaned over and called to me, "Climb in. I'll drive out to the foothills and let you take over. There won't be anyone else out there today." She was referring to the gasoline rationing our country was enduring. No one would be taking a scenic mountainside tour.

Off we set through the fertilized desert, across the big San Joaquin River to the Rockies.

So it was I found myself behind the steering wheel on a narrow mountain road which climbed itself up the side of the foothills of the Rockies. Debbie had shown me how to manage the clutch, gear shift, brakes, and reverse gadget.

"Don't worry about having to find room to pass someone, Anne." She told me. "We won't see anyone else up here today. They just don't venture out this far. And remember, I'm here right next to you, and I'm not going to let you drive too fast or venture off the road. George and Ed expect us home in time to fix their dinners."

What a time we had as I guided our little '36 Ford up the narrow road as it hugged the rocky mountain on Debbie's side and absolutely nothing on mine except thousands of feet of space. Ahead I could see what looked like the road's end, but I learned such views merely meant there would be an abrupt turn to the right as the road clung to the mountain side. We made it to the top.

Debbie and I climbed out. "Look out there, Anne. Can you see the dam on the San Joaquin? Remember the day we were out there soaking out feet in it and we heard someone cough?"

I laughed. How well I remembered. "Oh, yes, all those GIs who emerged from their hiding place in the trees. How they talked about their commander and how, if they weren't out of bed at seven in the morning when he arrived, he flipped their beds over. They were talking about my Ed! When I asked him about it, he confirmed what they had said. After all, he's in charge."

Standing there with Debbie and looking out over the San Joaquin valley reminded me. I had to make it to the base if we were to fix our dinners. Since that day, I have dearly loved driving no matter where I have lived

9

XOXOX

In July of 2009, the month before Mr. EUS and I met online as I sat before my computer I wondered, "Is the business world aware of the changes in life expectancy?" I shook my head in disbelief.

I decided to seek answers from businesses and colleges before plunging online to find my man. I would ask what research they were involved in which centered on the increasing longevity of the lives of men and women in today's world.

Then TV hadn't become inundated with ads for house security, devices for the elderly and such things as electric wheelchairs. These all followed the 2010 national census and its resultant study.

Only one positive response arrived out of forty requests I e-mailed out. It was from a small college in Kansas. A professor reported he had assigned a freshman class a research question. It asked whether the individual engaged in active sex. All those questioned were to be eighty or older. Sounds like some college prof, right?

It probably brought all kinds of enthusiastic reaction to his bunch of freshmen. However, the results amazed them all. More than 75 percent were sexually active. Considering the variety of health problems those in their eighties endure, I was amazed. I imagine the college freshmen were shaking their heads.

I had absolutely no reason not to launch my ship the very next morning. I suspected each would prove to be an absolute individual. None would be even similar. No two would be living next door to each other but rather, miles and miles apart.

Appearances would be unalike and their lives would have been traveled down different trails.

Despite the above, with very few exceptions, they all proved to be seven-second guys, most addressing the subject of sex in their very first letter. Maybe very subtle, but often outright and as a matter of fact, the subject would be brought up. So the Kansas College had done excellent research. All of us are aware within the last five years TV has suddenly blossomed out with sexual advice for we ancient ones here in America.

Of the over four hundred men I wrote, I'll just share with you those who directly affected my journey. Each man was always only himself. Their ancestry, their life's path, and what kinds of women they had chosen to be with were unlike any other. Most had been married for years and couldn't find a way to continue living if they were to be alone. Divorced men were few and far apart among the seniors online.

I learned from each the shape and size of cyberspace. Both are nonexistent. It is not like the world we live in which has roads, doors, windows, borders, and forms.

Remember my exchange of letters with Mr. EUS? It was then I opened the daily online series sheet of possible correspondents. Six men were listed. Just thinking back to that summer overwhelms me. I found myself on a journey I never ever could have envisioned. Nothing in my long life of eighty-six years had even hinted at the world out beyond me.

Before online dating, I'd taken the typical growing up path of all girls of my generation. I didn't speak out unless spoken to. This was a rule parents used to keep peace and order in their households. I ate everything on my plate or went to bed hungry. After all, my mother had taken the time to prepare the food, and Father thought we should respect her efforts.

The number of men presented to me each day overwhelmed me. I cancelled one of the online groups I had joined to trim the number down.

Earlier, after Mr. EUS had slammed his door on my overtures, I had received a "Want to write?" invitation from a man in Texas.

While I was spending time in Malaysia, I was traveling to Austin, Texas, to visit Will. His was one of the profiles finding their way onto my computer in early July, once I took that first plunge. His photo was so awful it caught my eye right off the bat. By that I mean one could hardly see him underneath his "pulled way over his eyes" cap plus dark glasses.

A second was available by another click. In it, he was atop a horse staring down at me. Immediately I smelled a big doubt. This was no Texan cowboy. They wear broad brimmed hats, not baseball caps. And where were the boots? No, this was a city guy out on a horse pretending he was a real Texan.

As our friendship grew, I learned I had been right on the money with my deductions. However, and wonderfully so, Will was an amazing man who reached out to me in every way he could. He was talented, even able to share with me his skills with editing. He was a pro at it all.

Over our first weeks, we were online together every day, learning who we were, had been and hoped to become in our life yet to come. During WWII, he had worked for a space company in Texas as their confidential business correspondent. I was fascinated with his enormous vocabulary he shared with me.

His enthusiasm was a glowing campfire steadily moving its deep warmth throughout me. The fun part in all this time together was the obvious fact he was yet another seven-second man. Yet his first short note to me was a turnoff. Not my age, either. He wrote,

Anne,

You look and sound delightful. I wish that I didn't live half a world away (in Austin, TX).

Will

It seemed to me I had another Mr. NY with his 639 reasons. What was wrong with the guys online? Where was their sense of adventure? Hadn't they heard of airplanes? Or trains? Or motor bikes? Or pedal bikes or skates? Or maybe they didn't have driver licenses.

And he had the guts to send me a picture of himself seated in the saddle of a real horse!

Yet he was online. Supposedly driven by loneliness and the never-ending second thought, the gift called a sex drive, with no intention of getting off his rear to explore the territory as his ancestors must have done for him to be where he was.

Those poor people had to travel through all kinds of weather, territory, and even hostile Indians to make it to Texas. It was all done on horseback or wagon, and he was telling me 1,500 miles was a problem?

It was beyond my understanding. It was as if those knights in shining armor were standing ready to fight but using distance as their shield; their protection against whoever might presume to enter their territory. Couldn't they understand every day they allowed to disappear was one day less they had to live? I suddenly felt sorry for Will who called himself online "APrinc4U."

Often when I tried hard to make something work, it seemed nothing I did was helpful. Then the unexpected happened and my problem was solved. This was exactly what Will did for me a few days later. In a short two sentence note he sent his very own e-mail address, asking me to use it to write him. And he asked for mine in return.

His idea was wonderful as we left the online "mail" service for our daily contacts. Our letters were e-mails resulting in a feeling of great, lasting friendship and intriguing secrecy. His became long as he slowly told me the story of his life. Unlike most of our generation, he had chosen to retire at fifty-five to leave Texas for the Rocky Mountains and ski country.

He explained, "I left our four college-educated adult children, two boys and two girls, back in Texas. Then with my Jean, we built a home and redid our way of living. We both became avid skiers; I took on becoming a ski instructor having a great time teaching others the 'how' of skiing, especially the younger girls!"

With my background as a wife whose husband had managed a ski area, I shared my experiences in the world of skiing.

"Oh, Will, how well I know what you are talking about. Ed lost his wonderful job as manager of the Port of Toledo in the summer of '61. Not because of anything he did or didn't do but because the Cleveland firm he worked for used him to cover up something they had done that hurt one of their customers, the US government.

"There we were with four children. The oldest was ready to start high school the coming fall, and we had to move way up into the northern part of Michigan's Lower Peninsula to manage a small ski area my brother had purchased. I was heartbroken to have to leave our families, those we knew and what had become our wonderful home—the one my father had helped Ed build as a result of my winning the McCall Magazine national contest on post WWII homes. Twenty-five thousand dollars in those days was a pile of money to suddenly be given. Like $250,000 today! I was in my last year at Fresno State."

As our stories continued, they were about my tiny Michigan ski area and his were about one of the West's major large areas. Mine included food preparation rather than teaching, but both were filled with fun stories.

His ended a terrible mess. In their fifth year, Jean, an alcoholic, was diagnosed with cancer and withdrew from skiing. To compound their problems, Will, only sixty, experienced a terrible ski accident. It left him unconscious for days. During this time, Jean died and was buried.

The resultant disbelief and despondency all but destroyed Will. He swore, "I'll never visit a doctor again as they are determined to keep me alive in ways I can't take." Obviously they had succeeded. And yet I understood why Will secluded himself in his apartment.

He wrote, "I go out once a month for supplies and walk each evening to one of three restaurants for my dinners, 365 days a year. My two sons visit to watch football every Sunday afternoon. One daughter lives on the Pacific coast and the other, who was responsible for my commitment to a mental hospital, is on my "no speaking" list although living in Texas.

As Will wrote of his life, two things happened. First I knew our friendship was genuine. Secondly, I came to understand how gently life had treated me despite the deaths of our children. It had been such a gentle time for both Ed and me. I understood Will and I would never have time together outside of cyberspace because of his attitude about the miles between us, yet we deeply appreciated our discovery of each other.

I asked him, "Will you call me on the phone?"

"You want me to call?"

"Yes, I'd love to hear your voice."

There was no answer. Suddenly my phone rang. Putting it to my ear, I said, "Hello, is that you, Will?"

I heard the deep voice of a man with a Texan "cowboy" drawl. I immediately pictured Will on Cinnamon's back, dark glasses and cap. Our conversation rambled on and on.

Finally as we were ready for good-byes, Will said, "Darling, I won't be calling again. I don't like to talk on a phone." Then he proceeded to explain why.

"It doesn't give me the time I desire to figure out what my answer should be."

I had never thought about telephones in this light but had to admit he was right on the money.

Then he surprised me with a request, "Sweetheart, do you have a Web cam?"

"What's that? A camera?" I asked. Then I added, "If it is, I don't. All I have is an ordinary one."

"If I send you the money to buy one, will you? I'd love to be able to sit here when I'm online with you and look at your beautiful face and more. I'll look into how much I need to send off to you. Will you get one for us?'"

So it was his check arrived and I purchased the camera. When I took his check in to deposit it, I noticed all his Texas information was on it as well as XOXOXO in large print on the lower left "What is this check for" line. The teller who I knew very well didn't comment!

10

Nearby

Over the years, the unexpected and the unexplainable have slapped me across the face more than once. Back when I was in my fifties, I really got smacked. I told you about the time Mother said she was praying to die every single morning all because of my father's death four years earlier. I had thought she was living happily in their comfy apartment.

My mother was deeply religious. Our entire childhood years, Doc and I had been in Sunday school every week. She even inserted favorite Bible quotes in her cookbook. These efforts on her part had succeeded in securely locking me within the house of the Lord. I could explain little, but deep within me understood some explanations were out of man's reach but true nevertheless.

There was no question in Mother's mind but that the Lord was there, waiting for her to join Dad. I have never heard anyone explain any of this. Yet I believe, just as my mother and dad had, that Ed is waiting for me somewhere.

This is what I thought of, as I thumbed through the day's profiles six months later. Although my interest had deepened considerably in a couple of the men I was communicating with, none had suggested he would like to meet me. Until this happened, I promised myself I would stay online.

Much to my surprise, there were two men from Michigan. Excitedly, I sent off my little "Hello" to the one who called himself "SXMusic." To have a musician beside me once again appealed. Ed had been both a barbershopper and choir member.

Dear SX,

I believe we have exchanged initial letters—sometime last week according to my notes.

I am not a petite woman—but am in excellent shape for my 5'7" height. But in all other ways, we are a match and I believe could have a wonderful relationship. Harrison isn't far away. We can arrange a meet somewhere in between for a chat and to get to know each other better than here online, if of interest to you. Otherwise writing works for me.

I am a writer, but laptops travel anywhere. And I am so Irish that I can claim the good looks, intelligence, health (no meds), and passion for life for which the nation is known.

Please write if interested.

Anne

SX's response arrived shortly after lunch.

Hi, Anne, that is a very nice message you wrote.

First I want to ask you how you feel about a guy being shorter than you.

You seem like a nice lady, and I would like to meet to at least see how much we really have in common. I have lost much of my hearing and wear aids, but other than that, I am still in pretty good health. My doctor says my heart is strong, but I do take medication for high blood pressure and high cholesterol.

I have been looking for a partner for a long time and even had a couple of ladies come here to live with me for a while, but that didn't work out.

If you would still like to meet, we could find a suitable place somewhere between your place and mine.

Let me know what you think.

Chuck

Dear Chuck,

Meeting you sounds wonderful. And my height won't bother me if it doesn't you—I have learned to live with it. When I was younger, I was 5'9" and taller than many men.

But I will be up front with you—I am a bit old-fashioned and "moving in" would never happen with me—for me there is a lot more about being with a man than the bedroom scene no matter how much fun it can be.

So, if I haven't thrown a wet blanket on this meet, please let me know where you would like to do it and when—sounds exciting.

Anne

The letter, which flew back, was no surprise. A disappointment yes, as I really would have liked to experience a meet with one of the online men. In my mind's eye, I could more or less script the event, but at the same time, I knew from experience what one envisioned seldom materialized as expected. Chuck's letter read,

Dear Anne,

I think we have run into a snag. I have always believed that sex is an important part of a relationship if both people care for each other and are willing. Apparently you are not one of those people. You said in your profile that you are romantic and that made me think that you would still enjoy sex. At eighty-three, I can still enjoy it once in a while. In my opinion, sex is not dirty but is beautiful. I guess we are not so much alike, after all.

Chuck.

Obviously, Chuck did not find it necessary to have too much in common with whomever he met as long as they shared his philosophy about sex. I can just visualize the bottle of "Stick-it-up" stimulant on his medicine cabinet shelf. Not that I felt the use of it was wrong, but on a 24/7 basis, I thought it would become pretty wearing. There were other great things, like a good book, great food, a walk along the lake, a hand of bridge—oh, you know—that I would have preferred wedging in once in a while.

I sent him a short "Best wishes as you search further" reply. But then I couldn't resist adding a PS.

"PS. Maybe if you took a little more time developing a relationship based on common interests and enjoyments with the women who you attract, they wouldn't move out in a few weeks. Anne"

I occasionally contacted a man online only to learn he had happily found his woman. You could hear the excitement and disbelief in his words. This was true for George. His new love lived just a block from his home in a large Texas City. Onliners from cities covered with apartments sheltering thousands of people, many of them singles, have an obvious advantage on the mileage issue. George and his new friend lived right down the street from each other but had to stroll into cyberspace in order to meet. Amazing.

11

Tuning the Fiddle

The entire summer and fall of 2009, I was tied to my computer. I remember my disbelief over the number of correspondents I found myself involved with. I laughed when I recalled my decision to join three online dating services to be able to find enough men to accomplish my goals. One would have been more than enough.

Between answering incoming letters and reaching out to those I had not written, plus endeavoring to keep each correspondent neatly filed in his own folder, was so much work I found myself spending an incredible twelve hours a day online. I had no time to be lonesome. Phone calls and chats filled my evenings.

The biggest surprise was Sunday's volume. If you stop and think about it, you'll realize for many Sunday has the most available free time for the things weekdays won't allow. I was completely fascinated by the world I had invaded.

Back then I was only eight-six years old. Today I feel no older, but I certainly know I am wiser. Unlike our world, there are no breathtaking valleys, towering mountains, or rumbling rivers in cyberspace. All this is what we expect to see about us but is not there. There is nothing. No land, sky, tree, flower, or bird.

The atmosphere online is provided by others. No two are alike; the men I met were unbelievable in their depth, dreams, experience, and desires. Each is another in many ways. They have also entered this new world forewarned of its dangers. Yet within themselves, they harbor needs requiring solution. They know of no other direction to move to solve their deep feelings of need—

to throw loneliness away. I suspect the family and friends of quite a few had no idea they were online dating.

Whether man or woman, the goals are surprisingly the same. They aren't shopping for a new car, tickets for a great vacation, good seats at a sporting event, or some personal treasure such as a ring or a fabulous dress. They all are seeking companionship to replace a loss.

For me, it was my Ed. What I had to learn was that I wouldn't find another Ed. I would find my treasure. But he would be a man nothing like what I'd had for those wonderful sixty-five years.

During the four months between July and October 2009, the variety of men with whom I exchanged e-mails was beyond belief. Thinking back, there are those who remain in my mind in a manner I doubt I'll ever cure. They were so special. None resembled the imaginary men I was so heartedly warned by friends and relatives not to involve myself with online.

One was a US Supreme Court justice retired happily on a Florida farm with his beloved dog. Another was a retired World War II navy deep-sea diver in Utah who was still occasionally taking on such work after having done it his entire life. Again the miles between us closed the doors.

There were authors, playwrights, TV programmers, and many, though in their eighties, who were actively engaged in their favorite sport. A Midwesterner who had spent his career as the owner of a trucking line offered me the opportunity to join him on a trip to Reno, Nevada, for a couple weeks of fun. He had kept one of his large cross-country trucks to use for such journeying and didn't want to do it alone.

I couldn't blame him, although I had to refuse. Reno held no interest. I admit I was somewhat suspicious of the seven-second thinking that was probably going on in his mind. Being of the era I was, I had promised myself I would only crawl in bed with a man after he proposed to me.

A neat ex-high school math teacher joined me online for a few weeks. Living in eastern Texas, he was four or five miles out of town. He was rare as he was not a seven-second thinker. At least he didn't hint or talk about it. His conversation was about his vegetable garden with a rattlesnake and his garage, which he was trying to motivate himself to clear out. It was bursting with tools he no longer used.

He was so personable visiting him online was just like sitting beside him on his front porch swing. But again, I was certain the miles between us made any other kind of relationship out of the question.

And Dude, who lived west of my granddaughter out in Tulsa, taught me a valuable thing for which I am grateful. After his complaint, I stopped sharing my Ed with other men online. Yes, Dude taught me the reason he decided not to drive down to see me while I visited Laura was because I talked about my Ed in my letters all the time. I wasn't ready to be online looking.

It was late October when Clayton came online. Again, I found myself writing to a man I never dreamed I would find. He was a retired Methodist minister, an army chaplain in the Korean War, and had his doctorate degree in psychiatry. His life had been in the pulpit, as a college professor, psychiatrist, and international broker.

The second day, he asked. "Can I call you this evening, Anne? I have some things I want you to know about me— not for you to learn later down the road."

We exchanged phone numbers and set seven as the call time.

That evening I found my mind blown away when he shared with me his private life. He had been married five times! Yes, the minister had five wives!

Three of his wives had died of cancer. Another had run off with his best friend during her menopause years. After he returned from the war in Korea, his first wife left to care for her mother who had become a quadriplegic. She had never come back.

Anne Thurston

Their two little daughters stayed with her to eventually become mathematic college professors.

In his disbelief and sorrow, Clayton returned to his army chaplaincy for an additional four years. There he met his second wife, a captain in the air force.

When I entered his life, he was in a puzzled state of mind because the online site had sent him my profile even though he no longer belonged to it or paid it dues. He was so taken with me he explained it to himself by accusing the Lord of interfering in his life one more time. I didn't know it then but this very same thing would affect me in a manner which caused me to think of the Lord also.

I think part of his fascination with me was the fact that both a son and daughter of mine, Tom and Nancy, were pastors as well as my son-in-law, Paul, and my grandson-in-law, Josue. Clayton also had received his psychiatric degree from a Detroit college, so he knew my state of Michigan well.

But the most wonderful surprise for me was his age. Clayton was nine days older than me. He was the first man I'd met online who was as old as I was, let alone older. Within a week, he was sending me his sermons to edit. His telephone calls became scheduled. Each evening, seven days a week, my phone rang at 7:00 p.m. We enjoyed each other's talk for well over a half hour. Somehow to him, the miles between North Carolina and Michigan had no bearing on our interest in each other.

I sent him a copy of *The Book of Anne*, the memoir I'd published in 2008. It told the story of Ed's and my raising our three orphaned grandchildren when we were seventy and sixty-nine years old. It was about the amazing gift it was to both of us as it offered no time to grieve over our daughter, Mary's, death and that of her husband, Pat, plus the death of our son, Tom. We were blessed with a life not many people experience.

In anticipation of Clayton's evening phone calls, I often sent him an e-mail question asking him to answer. One day I asked,

"Would you describe what it is men are looking for online in a woman, and vice versa?"

I was certain his answers would help me understand men better. I couldn't really believe my brother's seven-second explanation. Clayton had taught family relations at the college level in Pennsylvania. The telephone rang right on the money—seven o'clock.

"Anne, Clayton. How are you this evening, dear?"

"Just fine, Clayton. It is great to hear your voice."

Laughter. "And I feel the same about hearing yours." More laughter. "I sat down to write you the answers to your questions but decided it would be much easier to talk to you about them. First, let's start with the men.

"Anne, that one is simple. It is all about their masculinity. Their need to prove to themselves it is still there. Thus you often hear of men in their fifties and even sixties who are after younger women. It is their way of proving to themselves they still have what it takes. Remember the recent story about the governor of North Carolina, who was a candidate for the vice presidency of the country? Well, all he was doing was trying to assure himself he still had what it takes.

"Now in older men like me," he went on, "we still wonder. Even though I can only actually do anything about it once or twice a month, it is still important to me. Anne, a man always has his pants halfway around his knees."

As I listened to that doctor of psychiatry who had had his own marriage counseling practice in addition to five marriages, I found myself finally believing what my brother, Doc, had told me, three months earlier. It was exactly what men like Will and Jack had been backing up in their letters. I couldn't believe that at eighty-six, I was primarily a sex object to men of any age.

Did that make me centerfold material? In my artist's eye, I arranged myself provocatively. But Clayton was continuing,

"Now, Anne, at the same time, men are also looking for a woman with whom they can have a deep interest leading to respect. They often are not conscious of this. She must have those qualities that stimulate a man's interests as he fits her into his life. He must come to love her for these as well as her physical attraction to him."

Then he laughed heartedly and said, "Now women are entirely a different story. The reason for their searches is all about finding security. Many of them will attract a man and marry him only for his money, take it, and leave."

"Clayton, that is not at all true. I would never choose a man for his money. That is a very rude thing to say."

"I said many women. I did not say you would do this. I know you would not. But you are not the usual woman. That is why I am attracted to you. I knew right away when I saw your picture and read your letter you were not the typical woman, far from it."

I'd been angry, but the feelings simmered down somewhat. Still, Clayton was not clear of the woods with me. I felt he was way off base, just another typical male who misjudges the feminine half of his world. I was hurt and also disappointed in Clayton.

He seemed oblivious, that's one of the advantages of online relationships I suppose.

Continuing he said, "Now the other thing about women is they need to say to men what it is about themselves which is of interest. They must show the man exactly what he will find in her which will intrigue him forever. Every man and every woman have different interests, and it is here they will then fall in place. It is then men find the respect they seek. If they don't, they pull away."

As our conversation continued, I refrained from returning to his comments on women. I had learned to shut my mouth and think before I got too engaged in a dispute. As Clayton's prejudiced take on women loomed in my mind throughout the evening, I finally looked at the word Clayton used—*security*. I thought about its meaning and its synonyms.

Suddenly I knew what the word implied to him and understood its meaning had metamorphosed into an almost different form of security than yesterday's generation understood.

In those days, a woman's husband sheltered her within the security of a home he may well have built himself from timber growing on his land. He dug the ground in which she would plant vegetables and tend them. He hunted the animals they would eat. He dressed and prepared them for her use.

Natural phenomena such as floods, tornadoes, hurricanes, and other natural disasters caused the husband to rescue his wife and children. It was he who stood guard over what was theirs against criminals and marauders.

His arm around her shoulder assured her she would be safe as long as he was at her side. I had to admit today the husband can supply many of these protections through the money he earns— thus women see their man's money a big plus.

As our lifestyle mushroomed to include many desired things, the need for larger amounts of money beckoned today's women. Yes, Clayton did know women. I knew I had to tell him when we talked next I understood his words. I had the opportunity the very next night when he called.

He laughed and said, "Anne. I remember one of my marriage counseling cases. It fits in with the man and woman discussion we had yesterday. A middle-aged couple came in seeking advice on their desire to separate. I asked what seemed to be the main cause for their desire to divorce. The woman spoke up immediately. In an angry tone, she complained that her husband wouldn't consider stopping having intercourse with her. She had had enough.

"I knew immediately what the problem was. I dismissed her and asked the husband to remain with me. I explained to him over fifty percent of marriage failures in our country were due to the husband not taking the time to include his wife in the sexual act. I then showed him technical drawings of the female vagina and surrounding areas. My next step was to show him how to tune the fiddle before endeavoring to play it.

"I sent him home with the assignment to put in place that evening what I had shown him. He was to return to my office the following day to report his results.

"The next afternoon, he was once again seated in my office. He reported to me he followed my advice closely. But his efforts had failed as he could not keep his wife still long enough to have his own fun."

I laughed. Clayton's words made sense. I had long suspected way too many men didn't understand it isn't just about their feelings. Why should a woman want to continue such action for their entire lives? Men have to tune the fiddle. The better job they do, the greater their reward. My husband always did, and I never wanted him to stop.

12

Not Alone

Between Clayton's calls at seven and Will's chat at nine, I was no longer lonely. The two men kept my world alive. Then in September, I was in for another surprise.

Darleen, a young member of a national women's group, Women on Fire, invited me to attend a tea the group's local branch was holding. Hard to believe, but just five years ago, I was not one to voluntarily attend such gatherings. I had been shy all my life, and such events usually scared me off. This was especially true when the group was entirely all women. I simply did not understand their conversations, way of life, and perspective of the world about them. It all was scary.

Ed had understood all this and made a practice of always going out shopping with me and attending any social event he felt I should show up at. My shyness never stood between me and any of the service projects I did, such as getting the library reopened or serving on the school board or helping create Boyne's Artist Cooperative and Writers' Circle. And of course, the new schools were a result of my dad's house designing. My shyness only reared itself during social times. It felt in place not when I was working with groups but rather with only one person.

Even grocery shopping found me wanting Ed along in case someone wanted to stop and talk to me. He always had something to say to whoever might stop us to say "Hello." I did begin to come out of my shell a little bit as his illness progressed, and I had to venture into the grocery all alone.

Eventually, it was one of the men I'd meet online, who almost overnight inspired me to just toss most of my shyness away. It happened as I observed him approach a stranger in the grocery store to ask a question. Maybe it was just to ask an absolute stranger, "What in the world is that T-shirt of yours talking about?" They both ended up laughing and friendly. Mimicking him, I lost my shyness. But this was down the road.

But when Darleen offered to pay my way ($90) to the tea, I found it impossible to refuse. Thank heavens I went! I was in for a wonderful surprise.

Held in a small top floor room of a high Traverse City hotel, it was beautiful. Lake Michigan stretched out to its horizon below, just as the Pacific and Atlantic oceans do for so many coastal American cities. The tea was accompanied with delicious yummies. Merely fifteen of us were grouped around the table. Lovely vases of flowers decorated our conversation.

It was no surprise to find myself the oldest woman in attendance by far. I knew then my age was probably the reason Darleen invited me. I was a novelty. Darleen wanted to tease others about my age, to see if they could guess it.

After the planned part of the tea, we were released to move about and visit with each other. Darleen grabbed my arm and led me across the room to introduce me to one of the older middle-aged women.

"Martha," she called out. "I want you to meet my friend, Anne. She lives up north of here and writes and paints. How old do you think she is?"

I was ready for her question. I had known Darleen would pull this on me. She had done it before. I nodded my head at Martha and smiled my hello, saying, "Oh, don't let Darleen embarrass you. I'll tell you my age."

Immediately Darleen put her hand over my mouth and said, "No way, Anne. Martha has to guess."

Obviously aware what was up, Martha responded, "So Anne is older than she appears? Well, instead of saying about sixty-five as I probably would have, I will up that a bit. How about seventy?"

Laughing happily, Darleen shook her head. "Good try, Martha, but eighty-six is correct."

To my surprise, Martha asked me, "How old do you think I am, Anne?"

Surprised at her question, I studied her face. I thought she was probably about forty-five, but I upped it to fifty. To my amazement, she was sixty-three! This led us into a great conversation, which still causes me to shake my head even now, five years later.

In her younger years, Martha had become a movie producer in Hollywood. She named some well-known actors whom she had directed. I shook my head in amazement. As the years rolled by, she became wealthy, acquiring a beautiful home in Hollywood. Yet she found no husband. Her board of directors, all men, bored her with their habit of not gathering until nine in the morning and all with a drink in their hand.

The day came when she had had it with her single life. She took herself to a nationally renowned therapist for women located in Los Angeles. The doctor's advice was to go online to search for the man she desired. I couldn't believe my ears.

Martha did and found him. He was a doctor in Michigan. Retired early from the medical profession in Detroit, he had decided to return to his grandparents' farm near Alpena in northern Michigan. There he was happily restoring it as it stood beside a small river wondering through the hills and forests.

For both of them, having the money for numerous cross-country flights, the relationship grew into marriage. Her happiness glowed on her face. Once again, I was confronted with the problem of distance. These two had their solution in their pocketbooks, but that wouldn't work for many others. Even when the man has the money, he may be reluctant to spend it on something so uncertain. What if she didn't turn out to be what he'd hoped for?

I returned home from the tea completely convinced I was on the right track. I would find my man. Sure enough, when I opened my computer, there they were in my e-mail, more possibilities, just waiting.

About a month later, in November, my decision to find a man for myself was reinforced. Comfortably stretched out on my living room couch, I had my nose in one of Nicholas Sparks's great books unaware of the time. Oh, I knew it was well after midnight but was determined to learn it's ending if I stayed up a couple more hours.

Suddenly a rough pain hit me in the jaw. I felt like I had been socked. Wow!! I instantly recalled a recent bit of reading I had done about the different types of pain women suffered rather than men experienced during heart attacks.

I couldn't believe the pain. It was worse than anything I had ever experienced including surgeries and falls. Everything in my living room disappeared into nothingness as I held my jaw in my hands. Then slowly I began to feel pain creeping into my upper arms and into my chest slowly.

I shook my head and told myself, "Anne, you are having a heart attack. You are alone. You have to get out of this chair and take care of yourself. You have promised yourself and everyone else you would do so. Now move."

Laying my book aside, I got up and found an aspirin in the bathroom. My upper arms and chest as well as my face were a bit achy. Gosh! I told myself. You are having a heart attack. This is exactly what your family worries about happening to you living alone. Now is the time to prove to them they have no need to worry. You are perfectly able to drive myself to the hospital.

Grabbing my coat, purse, and car keys, I was out of the apartment building in a couple of minutes. As I climbed into my little Ford, I saw a police car slowly approaching the parking lot.

It was not unusual for the local police to receive a complaint about a late-night disturbance in one of the apartments. He slowly drove through the area between the two rows of parked cars. The drive was down the middle between parking spots.

Right behind my parked red Focus, he slowly came to a halt and sat, looking and listening.

I couldn't believe he had parked exactly behind me. There was no way I could leave to get over to Charlevoix and the hospital. Obviously I had to ask him to move. I jumped out of my car and headed back to his.

My unexpected rap on his car window completely startled him. As he rolled it down, I asked, "Would you please move enough so I can back my car out? I need to head to the hospital as I think I might have had a small heart attack."

Looking at me, he asked, "Did you think of calling an ambulance?"

"Oh, not really. I took an aspirin and am feeling okay, and why wake them up?"

"But have you thought perhaps you might have another one on the way to Charlevoix and hurt someone else?"

Naturally I hadn't thought up such a possibility. I agreed to have him put the call in. We waited ten or fifteen minutes for the ambulance's arrival. I climbed myself into its rear end, crawled up on the bed-table, and we headed off.

Once admitted into the hospital, I was tested thoroughly and then sent off to bed for the rest of the night.

The following morning, I woke up feeling great. When Dr. Jim arrived beside my bed, I asked, "I feel great. I didn't have a heart attack, did I?"

"You are right, Anne. What you had we refer to as an improbable heart attack. This is because all your body functions such as heart rate, blood pressure, et cetera, were perfectly normal. Your heart is fine."

I was in great shape. My heart was great. Some old worn-out vein or artery of mine had merely collapsed.

Now, five years later, I continue taking the same little daily pill to control this and feel great.

A couple weeks after all this, my granddaughter Laura in Iowa called to ask me to join her family along with her brother and sister at her home in Tulsa for Christmas. I was thrilled, but thought it wise not to share my hysterical trip to the hospital. She would probably advice me to stay put.

I could just hear her, "Oh, Grandma, take it easy and quit your driving. There is bus service in Boyne. I remember it."

Sitting here and remembering I have to admit the night of the hospital journey would have been far easier if I had had the man I was searching for right there beside me. There is nothing like your man's arm around you and his kiss on your face when the world takes off in an unexpected direction.

Yes, I am so thankful I was on my cyberspace journey despite all its ups and downs because the reward waiting for me would be beyond all my expectations.

13

Proposals

Before I set out to be with my family of grandchildren over Christmas in 2009, another strange thing entered my world. As I look back on it all today, I simply can't be 100 percent certain if I figured it all out correctly at the time, maybe not.

Of all the men I corresponded with back in those days, it was Will, my Texas editor, who pulled the rug out from under my feet. Yet despite doing so now four years afterward, he still checks in on me now and then. He is the only one of all those I corresponded with who does.

In early November of 2009, we had been corresponding with each other online four months. His fifteen hundred miles were still between us. For his own enjoyment, he said he was reading a minimum of two books a week. Belonging to one national book club after another, he obtained them easily right in his mailbox. No jaunts to the library for him. I was in awe of his vocabulary.

Earlier in the summer, he'd pleaded, "Darling, do me a favor please. Since you haven't read John Fowler's *Magus*, I wish you would—it's my favorite."

He envisioned himself as its Nicholas so deeply; he sent me an e-mail from "Nicholas" addressed to me. In it, Will, as Nicholas, shared the information about his beloved wife who had been an alcoholic, and dealing with that had been frustrating, yet he had never resorted to physical violence. Instead, even when she was at her worst, he simply held her in his arms.

I wrote back to 'Nicholas," telling him I was not at all surprised to read his story because Will was such a special man.

But let me go back to the unbelievable surprise Will pulled on me that November as winter was approaching. At least it was for me, maybe not for him way down in Texas.

Soon after we opened our usual nine o'clock chat one late October night, he asked, "Who's responsible for keeping your roads snow free during the winters?"

I explained, "We have an unbelievably gifted road commission. It's up and about in the wee hours of the mornings. Because of this, no overnight parking is permitted on our streets and roads. The exception is our town which has its own crew. The county group is also responsible for the state highways that cross it."

Will knew all about the various ski areas surrounding Boyne City. That had come up long before when I learned of his love for skiing and time in the Rockies as an ardent skier and coach. So his next question surprised me. It had nothing to do with snow plowing.

"Are there any apartments for rent there in Boyne?"

"Oh, yes. My dearest friend Grace rents one and calls it her home. It is just a block back from the lake. It has a wonderful view of the water and is the only apartment complex of all ours which boasts an elevator."

As I answered the thought that he might be considering a visit during the ski season worked itself into my mind.

His answer took it further than this.

"Could I buy one?"

"What are you saying, Will? Are you thinking of moving up here so I can see you? What about your family there in Texas?"

"Anne, you wouldn't be visiting me. We would be in the apartment together. Remember, for years I was way off in the Rockies and my kids were all college graduated back in Texas—it is you I want to be with."

The thought of having such a wonderful man at my side for the years to come overwhelmed me. We could write together! I responded emotionally. "Oh, Will, I can't believe all this is happening. I will visit a realtor and gather the information which will answer all your questions. Just wait until you see what you'll have in your hands, honey. Oh, my darling, you are making my dream come true!"

I also promised to send him all the ski hill information I could find at our chamber of commerce.

I can't remember whether I slept that night or not. I thought of our writing and how he would be with me to work on it all. We would become coauthors. I gathered all the promised information the next day by visiting my dear realtor friend Dick Fish and mailed it off in one-day mail.

It arrived the next day, Saturday. Will was excited about it all. His e-mail told me which apartment he was going to go after and how hard it was for him to believe he once again would be living in the part of the world where winter brought snow. He added to this his excitement about my being with him.

I understood his excitement. My years in California and on Guam taught me life to be complete had to include winter. To this day, I relish it even though most around me moan and groan about the cold, the snow digging and the slippery roads. The beauty and the cold air bring a stimulus into life I can't give up.

A Sunday e-mail arrived to tell me he might be late getting on chat as his sons were coming over to watch football in the afternoon and evening. He was enticed by all the literature I had sent.

Back in August, Will had come online with a suggestion.

"Anne, it's time we went on chat together."

"What are you talking about?" I replied.

"It's a way to be together online that is more like talking to each other than writing. As soon as I write you a question or share some news, you can immediately answer me." He plunged right in to the process.

I was to look to the left side of my screen and click on Chat. Immediately a small box appeared in the lower right hand corner of my computer screen.

"I have the chat box in front of me, Will. What do I do next?"

Even as I asked, I noticed words appearing across the box. Will was writing me. "Hi there, beautiful. Answer me."

I immediately typed, "Well, hello there, handsome." And we were off.

Night after night, we chatted for two hours. Will believed eleven o'clock Michigan time was late enough for me to be out of bed. At eleven, our conversation would change dramatically. It was then the seven-second Will appeared.

For another fifteen minutes, he would tell me in detail how he would stimulate me once we were in his bed together. Obviously he tuned his fiddle. What a time he had! And supposedly I was right there with him having the time of my life. Finally he would say, "My love, you are an unbelievable woman. I am so glad you are in my arms. Go to sleep now and have wonderful dreams. I love you so much."

So I waited from our usual "on time" of 9:00 p.m. on into the evening. No Will chat or e-mail arrived. I hung in until 1:00 a.m. and gave up. I hoped he wasn't having one of his "not feeling too well" sieges again.

Maybe the excitement had triggered one. Will had had them off and on since his ski fall. But he refused to go near a doctor. He'd had his fill of them unfortunately. I'd check in with him the next day.

The days passed one after another. It was then I woke up to the fact that no one in his family knew I existed just as no one in mine had any idea one of the men I was so happily corresponding with was in Texas or that his name was Will. Not even my Nancy knew of Will. Oh, she knew of some of the men. She knew about

Clayton, the minister. He intrigued her with all his marriages. She had even been at my house during a couple of times I had been online with Mr. Malaysia but never with Will.

This amazing friend of mine who had just decided to come north so we could finish our lives together could have died. How was I ever to know?

Today I have been shown how to locate others through my computer and learn if they are living or dead. Five years ago, I tried the only idea I could conceive.

I located the telephone number of the business office of the apartments Will lived in. I called and a young woman answered. I asked, "Is there any way to check Will's apartment to see if he is there? I am an online friend with him and haven't been able to get him to answer my e-mails for over a week. He has health problems, and I am deeply concerned about him."

Her answer was what I dreaded. "Oh, I'm sorry but I am not permitted to give such personal information out." Then without hesitating, she told me, "But I understand your concern and I will go to see if anyone is in the apartment."

Shortly she called me back to tell me, "Yes, there is someone in the apartment. I am not at liberty to say anything more. I hope this helps you."

In desperation, I called my brother. With tears in my eyes, I told him detail what had happened between Will and me. "Doc, what can I do to find an answer to all this?"

He answered immediately. There was laughter in his voice, yet it was stern and sympathetic. "Sis, I tried to warn you about the guys you would find online. Now you have. He simply has had his kicks and has decided to find someone else. Let him go. You've had your fun and you are still okay. Be thankful it isn't worse. Get off-line and forget having a man. Ed was yours for a long time. Be thankful and remember him."

In deep disappointment, I checked Will off my list. I convinced myself he was well but when his sons had been shown the pictures of Boyne and told of their father's plans to leave Texas and start a new life they shouted a big *no*. With their deep concern and love, they had leaned on their dad hard, convincing him such an idea was way beyond anything he should want to get himself in. He didn't know me, for heaven's sake! These were my thoughts.

The proposal I had so hoped to win online had been given and within hours yanked back. Slowly I backed away from such a happening. Knowing Will as I had come to, I couldn't believe his sons could wield enough opposition to stop him from arriving. He must be ill. My prayers went out to him. I simply could not accept my brother's words.

I reminded myself of the others I was coming so close to and not to let myself give up. Surely among all these exceptional men, I'd find one with whom my life would be wonderful.

Looking back, I remember my discouragement. And I understand it now. I simply had not fully embraced the possibilities and limitations of cyberspace. I was still thinking of it in terms of the world we live in day after day. It isn't the people who are any different; it is that they react to the world around themselves differently.

While in cyberspace, we are influenced by its isolation. We are somewhere we have never been. It is a world holding no resemblance to our world on earth. There is nothing to touch; nothing to see. If we reach out to touch something what we feel is here on earth, not in cyberspace. No, it is only in our minds, an area of our bodies scientists are still exploring.

As unreal as this all sounds, it does exist. And we react to it differently than we do to the world around us. We feel out of reach of those we write until we break our isolation with a telephone call or visit. Suddenly you have fallen out of cyberspace back into your own world and all its potential greatness or problems.

Close family members can offer terrible discouragement. For centuries, ones parent's money was dangled out in front of their children's face as their inheritance once the parent died. Among the wealthy, this can be enormous sums of money. Those who may not have quantities of money often have property which can be left and change the life of their reciprocates just as money would.

I ran into this eventually. It cost me not money but something far more valuable. But I can't jump ahead here.

During the month of November as I prepared for my Christmas visit to Tulsa, I couldn't stop hoping Will would come back.

He did, the week before I was to leave. There was Will on chat at 9:00 p.m. just as he had been for weeks. It was wonderful having him back to chat with. He seemed his old self during the entire time we spoke.

He never mentioned the preceding weeks he had not contacted me. Nor did he mention his decision to move to Boyne, purchase an apartment, wrap me in his arms and go skiing on a Michigan slope. It was never brought into our conversation. Not once. I did not ask any questions.

I found it impossible to bring the subject up. Something within me was silently defining his lack of communication as health related. I am certain it was based on the story he had told me about his ski accident and return to Texas after his wife's death in the Rockies. His hospital stay had been extensive.

Upon his release, his oldest daughter had taken him back to her Texas ranch. She had purchased a small house trailer for him to rest in and return to health. However the day came when she called the county sheriff to have him taken to a mental institution. She suspected he was about to attempt suicide.

It took Will ten days to convince the attending doctors his daughter's suspicions were absolutely not true. They released him. Instead of returning to his daughter's ranch, he relocated himself in the city campus apartment he was living in as he spoke. He swore he would never ever go to see a doctor again. He trusted none.

I came to the conclusion he had suffered another mental breakdown similar to the one which followed his wife's death during the time he could not be at her side. Perhaps the extreme excitement of his decision to be with me had triggered another mental problem. And once he survived the bout, its cause had vanished. He has no memory of his proposal. I knew this was possible. Our David had no memory of the entire month he was in the hospital following his head injury as a result of his slipping on the ice by his mailbox. And yet we had all been with him during our hospital visits. He doesn't remember them.

All this worked itself around in my brain. I prayed he would be all right, but even to this day, I have no certain answer. Yet I sincerely believe something erased his joyous plans to move north and be with me. His occasional contacts have been very sporadic, yet all Will. I am sorry we couldn't have been together. My help would have been his.

14

Look Ahead

My flight out to my granddaughter's in Tulsa landed me in front of a wild winter storm coming in from the east. It prevented my grandson, Patrick, from landing and caused his sister, Rachael, and her husband, Rutt, a shortened stay. However, I stayed for more than a week. It was wonderful to hold my little great-granddaughter, Natalie, in my arms.

Tulsa reflected the immense wealth the area has accumulated from oil. Huge homes stood in large groups behind locked gates. Yet the land itself did not look rich, appearing flat as far as the eye could search. Unlike Michigan's farm countryside, its fertility is underground in liquid man calls oil.

Although I had notified my online correspondents I would not be home for the holidays, Clayton continued to call me at seven each night. I had posted Laura's telephone number in my "Good-bye and have a wonderful Christmas" e-mail to my men. Will also "chatted" with me a couple of times.

My bedroom off the front entry hall was Josue's at home office so I had his computer to use. It was also the girl's playroom with Natalie's desk with its drawer full of crayons and paper. The two of us had busy art sessions.

After dinner, Josue carried the Christmas tree in for us to decorate. He had a corner to set it in next to the living room's big fireplace. My mind flooded of other Christmas trees. Natalie surprised me with her help. But then she is a little artist. Gabbi's time was yet to come about four years down the road.

Their big black curly dog tried her best to get her nose into all our work. She was only a year old and still a playful puppy and intrigued with all the hanging toys. I was filled with years of memories. Other homes, other family members, and yet there I was with my great-granddaughter. It was almost too much to believe.

Being in another part of our country for over a week and part of my Laura and Josue's life was a return to my long life of family beside me. The fact Josue's mother, father, and grandmother were also visiting for the holidays added to the feeling of being a whole person. They were from Brazil. Remember Josue and Laura met at college? His mother could speak English so was my interpreter when I wanted to say something to her mother or husband. Christmas day was held in Josue's sister's home about one hundred miles southwest of Tulsa. There I met even mote of his family. His two brothers and sister had all been sent to the United States to obtain their college degrees and as a result had elected to remain here.

His father is a doctor and manages a hospital in his hometown. Josue's mother almost has her medical degree also. I suspect she needed to find something to keep her busy after her four children moved to the USA. The food they prepared for our holiday dinner was so special. Many of the dishes were first timers for me.

All in all, having the time with Laura and hers helped me surmount the deep pit Will had unintentionally and unknowingly plunged me. It was hard to climb on board the plane to fly back to Michigan.

15

The Question

After such a fun time with Laura and her hubby, I reluctantly boarded my flight back home. Josue, the Brazilian student Laura met in their Kentucky seminary, was a wonderful Methodist minister in a large Tulsa church.

My Christmas visit had been exceptional as I attended all its celebration activities as his special grandmother. I was welcomed with outstretched arms and attended a very special Sunday school class of older generation members. They included me in their annual Christmas delicious dinner at a member's home. To this day, we remain friends.

Back home with Dude's disinterest and no one special waiting for me, I felt the loneliness of my empty apartment. I was once again, home alone. I missed Ed.

I was at my computer. It was a Sunday afternoon. In the process of writing to some new and some familiar men, I was discovering they'd all made this same observation. They were lonely for their loved ones just as I was.

Clayton, my online companion down in North Carolina, was the exception. He told me he was used to being alone. That was the result of his returning from the Korean War to discover his wife had left him to care for her mother. She had elected to take their two small daughters with her.

The girls had continued to live some distance away even after their mother's death. They were both college professors. They never gathered with him on special occasions. It was his congregation which helped fill the vacancy for him. That day our telephone conversations made a lot of difference to us both. We laughed a lot.

Not long after he asked me one evening, "Will you answer some questions?"

I assured him I would. "What are they about?"

He said, "You don't understand yourself. I believe can help you do so."

I immediately felt as if I was in a college classroom, and the professor was handing me an assignment. Cautiously I told Clayton I would try to answer his questions if possible. He assured, "You'll do fine."

"Anne, please write down what it is you consider to be your attributes."

I remember thinking, "What is this man up to?" Well, one way to find out is sit down and do the answers. I promised him I would e-mail them to him later that night or in the morning.

I felt I was doing a bit of homework as I diligently wrote down my answers; those things the Good Lord had given me. I listed my art ability, my writing, being a parent, a gardener, and so on. At the close, I reminded him that these were gifts of the Lord and had nothing to do with me.

All the time I wrote, I felt as if I was in the midst of some college course. Clayton was my professor. As for him, he fit the roll perfectly.

During the terrible disappointment over his beloved first wife, he had returned to college to earn a degree in oncology and also one in psychiatry. In his lifetime, he had been a minister, a university professor, had his own psychiatric clinic and brokerage.

He once shared with me he refused to accept menopausal woman or teenage girls as patients. He felt both of their minds at the time in life were beyond human understanding. I remember my rolling laughter.

Somewhere in the midst of all this, he had created an international brokerage dealing in major items such as gold, coal, oil, etc. With the aid of two partners, he'd earned millions of dollars. Most of it had been given to Duke University's theological college, his alma mater.

The next evening, he thanked me for my answers and said he was surprised I recognized I had so many areas of ability. However, it was his opinion that I was off base by crediting the Lord for them.

As the minister and professor he was, he explained to me, "Anne, you are correct. Your abilities are gifts from God, but if you did nothing with them, His gifts would benefit no one. No, you are the one who should receive the credit for what you do for others, not the Lord."

To this day, his words haunt me. I find myself aware of my gifts more than ever before, and at the same time strive harder than ever to use them to help others. Clayton changed my attitude about life. I find myself shaking my head about it all.

February 2010 arrived. Looking out my window at the snow one morning, I paused. It had been a year since Ed's death. My phone rang, shaking me out of my reverie. Much to my surprise, it was Clayton's voice I heard.

"Anne, my dear, I wasn't able to sleep last night. No matter what I tried I just couldn't. I finally got up and tried to understand what was preventing me from sleeping. It hit me. It was you. I couldn't sleep because I wanted you."

Then he popped the question. Yes, *the* question.

"Anne," he said, "will you marry me?"

There was a moment of dead silence.

Then I heard myself say, "Clayton, can you give me some time? I'll call you back in no more than an hour."

"I expected this might shake you up, darling. Yes, take the time you need."

16

Back and Forth

I can't tell you how long it took me to call Clayton back because I don't know. I only remember sitting there on my chair, phone in hand, staring out the window at the woods. My mind rolled itself over. With all he was and had been in his lifetime, how could I be so fortunate to have him seek me out? He thinks me so wonderful he can't live without me by his side?

I'm sure it wasn't anywhere near an hour for me to call back. "Yes!" I told him. "Yes, Clayton, I will marry you."

Clayton must have stayed right in his chair, too, phone in hand staring out his windows at his morning sky. The minute I rang, he picked up. When he heard my "Yes!" his joy was obvious.

"Clayton, I would so much love to be your wife from here on out," was what I told him and what I meant.

A surprise waited me. Knowing him as well I had come to, there should have been nothing unexpected when he replied he had arrangements made for my flight to come down and spend the Valentine's Day weekend with him in North Carolina. "I'll mail you your ticket. We'll attend a concert. I'll introduce you to my senior partner as minister at the church and attend an apartment gathering. I can't wait to introduce you to all my friends."

Clayton continued, "I have an apartment set aside for you and a car."

I felt like a twenty-year-old! There was nothing I needed to change or add to our time together. Clayton's part of being a well-organized businessman and professor was behind it all.

When I started out on this adventure to search for a man, I had promised myself I would spend no time with any one of them until I had an engagement ring on my finger. Yes, I am old-fashioned about this. But, even though Clayton had not done so, I saw no way his proposal would vanish into the air as Will's had. I had succeeded in my search for an end-of-life companion. And what a wonderful person he was despite all the bumps life had tossed his way. I had learned he had fallen in his living room and struck his head on the coffee table just two years before our online meet.

Stunned and hurting, he stumbled into his bedroom and stretched out on the bed as the pain increased. He passed out. Five hours later, his housemate arrived home to discover Clayton out of his world. He took him to the town's veteran's hospital. Three months later, he came out of his coma.

He had another year to wait to return home. This happened because one morning his nurse asked, "Do you intend to die in the hospital? Don't you think God has any more things for you to get done first? I think so."

As a result of her words, she left, saying, "If you need to use the toilet, you can get out of bed and do so. There will be no bedpan brought to you today."

Clayton heard her words and knew God had more for him to accomplish. He took the necessary steps and returned to his apartment a few days later. Since then, he had taken the nurse out for lunch every month in appreciation for what she had done for him. I was also to meet her.

I can vividly recall my son David's reaction to my call, telling him of my planned journey to visit Clayton. And why I was going.

He drove the one hundred miles between our homes to bring me a cell phone.

I asked Nancy and Paul to come up to be at my place to enjoy David's visit. They heard him say, "Mother, keep this in your pocket every minute of the time you are away. If anything should happen, call and I will be right there for you."

I accepted the phone knowing there was simply no way I could ease my son's worries. He had had no opportunity to get to know the amazing man I was going to marry. I saw the deep worry and concern on David's face. I so wished Clayton stood beside me so he and my children could have the opportunity to talk, ask questions, exchange thoughts, relax, and understand why I had said yes.

Nancy, knowing Clayton was a Methodist minister and of his many marriage experiences and the sad stories behind each Clayton had in his lifetime, was relaxed and even excited about his proposal. She tried her best to calm David's apprehensions, but he didn't ask for the phone back.

The few days I had between Clayton's proposal and the departure date he had chosen immediately began to evaporate. Like any woman, I enveloped myself in what I should take in my suitcase. After all, I wanted to look as beautiful as he imagined me from my online photo.

I drove the sixty some miles down to Traverse City to catch my flight. Sue Ellen, my Tom's widow and my daughter-in-law, met me. Helping board my flight, she waved and called out, "Have a great flight, Mom, and bring us back a photo of your to-be husband."

I remember so vividly my first glance at Clayton as I disembarked from my flight. Way down the hallway from the unloading area to the airport's front entry stood a little old man leaning on a cane in his right hand. He had told me he used a can for stability. I understood; my knees are my problem. They don't want to let me stand up once I'm seated. When his eyes spotted me in the crowd of passengers waving at others, his face broke into a huge smile. The aged look disappeared. There stood the man who was to be mine for the rest of our years. I never saw him as old after that moment.

As quickly as our legs would allow, we were in each other's arms. Oh, what joy! We started talking right away. "How was your flight, darling?" Next it was, "Where's your suitcase. I'll get it for you." The words never stopped until we were at his car's side.

Once he tucked me into his car, he slide into the driver's seat and further threw our late years away by pulling me to him and enveloping my face with kisses. We were like two teenagers so in love. The feeling was never to leave us, only expand. His words, whispered into my ear as he kissed, "Oh, my Anne, my wonderful Anne!" have never left me.

We stopped on the way to his apartment for lunch, never ceasing our conversation. Once home, he showed me all its rooms and sought my help in preparing an afternoon wine and goodies party for his church's senior pastor and his wife. Standing beside the little but long coffee table between his couch and two overstuffed chairs ready to clear off its surface, he said, "Anne, I am so anxious for Joseph and Arlene to get to know you. They think they do because of reading your book, but you are more than that." He gave me another hug and kiss and stood there smiling at me. Of course, I had my arms around him and a big smile on my face.

Remembering what it was he should be doing, he handed me the magazines on it he indicated I was to tuck them under one of the end tables by the couch. Then he led me with his hand holding mine into his tiny kitchen and began pulling things out of his refrigerator, which I could arrange on the coffee table.

I then suggested he add some of the flowers I saw out near his deck. He nodded his head yes, and we hurried outside to pick some. It wasn't long until Joseph and Arlene arrived. While we waited for them, we sat side by side out on the deck talking about where I was and was about to see. Neither of us was aware of anything else. The world was just ours.

Twenty-five years younger than Clayton, Joseph had been struggling with a tiny Methodist church there in town when

Clayton moved into the area and offered his help. Together he and Joseph had revived the church wonderfully.

Clayton looked upon this episode in his active life as proof the nurse had been correct when she urged him to continue living, God had had work for him to do. And he put me in this belief also. Obviously, God had wanted him to be with his Anne to love and care for her at his side.

I had a wonderful time in North Carolina. The weekend was way too short. Joseph and his wife, Arlene, arrived for the little afternoon party. Clayton had loaned them my book, *The Book of Anne*, which I had sent him. It was the story of Ed and my raising our three orphaned grandchildren. The minister and his wife were doing the same thing for an identical reason. Their divorced daughter had suddenly died and left her ten-year-old son with them. I met the son at the church service that Sunday. He was a high school freshman. After their good-byes, Clayton prepared supper for me, and then we headed out for the evening's concert.

It was wonderful, covering the entire stage in the big auditorium. Clayton once had been on the Baltimore Orchestra Board so had purchased exactly the correct seating. We were third row, left side of the auditorium. The pianist was directly in front of us as we listened to the music. Clayton sought my hand and held it. Leaning over, he whispered, "Anne, I love you more than I ever dreamed I could." It was wonderful to be a man's again.

I had a tour of my apartment after our evening out. It was two blocks from his and equally nice. Once inside, he searched out its bedroom and proceeded to fulfill his evening. I would say he had carefully planned it.

Reminding myself I had accepted his offer of marriage even though I had not received an engagement ring, I joined him in turning down the bed cover and sheets. Then as he disrobed on his side of the bed; I did the same on mine. Clayton had explained his prostate surgery to me sometime back when he discussed his health. We were both aware there was no hope of intercourse.

However, I was not to be concerned as he promised we would have wonderful times together in bed. Snuggled together and with a big smile on his face, Clayton whispered, "Anne, my dear, I am about to tune your fiddle. Are you ready?"

I murmured, "I'm your fiddle and ready to make music."

Thus he began to show me how this was all to take place. In his words, he "tuned" my fiddle. I laughed to myself as it brought back his tale of the patient he had helped learn to "tune the fiddle."

I had to admit, we had a riot together. Obviously it was enough to satisfy this man of so many marriages. He held me in his arms and murmured, "Oh, my unbelievable woman having you here with me is beyond my dreams. I know you have enjoyed every minute, too. I can't wait for tomorrow night." Reluctantly he rose out of bed to return to his own, promising me he would be back for me by nine in the morning.

"I'll be here to pick you up and we'll head out for breakfast before going on to church. I'll be with you for part of the service as I'm not to be the main speaker, but rather Joseph's assistant."

The church was not a giant city type but rather more like a small town's place of worship. Once in its door, I met a few members before Clayton plumped me down in a third-row pew. It was at the end of the service Clayton spoke to the membership, "I've committed myself to remarriage and am proud to introduce Anne Thurston to all of you." (His finger was pointing me out to them.)

"Will you stand, please, Anne, so my friends can welcome you into their lives also?"

I stood to acknowledge their kind welcoming hand clapping. I turned toward Clayton and shook my finger at him for what he had done. His eyes twinkled and his mouth spread into a huge smile as he winked at me.

After church and lunch, he drove me up into the Appalachian Mountains, which stretched out against the west side of his town.

It was beautiful. He located a small resort where he promised we would spend some time when we were back together.

In a little park on a hillside, we made wedding plans. Clayton was determined it should be in Michigan where my family lived. His family was too small and distant to worry about. Once winter was over, he would travel up to me and we would finalize our plans and carry them out. "Will June work for you, dear?" he asked. I nodded yes as we wrapped our arms about each other.

Later, in town, he took me to a residential area to see some beautiful apartment buildings. One with flower gardens and a lovely porch was owned by the Methodist denomination and would be available for him to purchase or rent. He asked, "Do you like it?"

I have to say, it excited me. I could tell it did Clayton. We both felt as if we were living in a dream world—one we had imagined but never believed could ever exist! As he had a key, we invaded the interior and became further excited about having it all as ours. Back in my apartment that evening, our cuddling and loving were more spontaneous than they had been the night before. Our day together had relaxed us both. We had become each others. He stayed beside me all night.

17

A Night to Remember

In the morning, we reluctantly crawled out of bed and stopped for a quick breakfast before driving to the airport about noon. Rather than saying good-bye, we talked about our spring and summer plans. It was hard to turn from his arms and our last kiss to go find my airplane. I was to fly to Washington, DC, and then to Traverse City, where Sue Ellen and my car would be waiting for me. It would then be a sixty-five-mile-drive home.

Inside at the terminal's counter, I was in for a terrible blow. An extensive snowstorm was entering the area from the south. The capitol's airport was being closed down completely. They could still get me onboard a plane for Chicago rather than Detroit. The following morning, I would be flown onto Traverse City. Chicago was my only choice if I was to leave, and I felt I should. Clayton had been completely unaware of the mess. I didn't go back out and share the news with Clayton. "Why worry him?" I thought. "I'll be okay."

Thus, it was I found myself in Chicago about an hour before midnight. My plane would leave at 6:00 a.m. the following morning. Having had nothing for dinner, I took time off to eat. Then I realized doing so had been foolish. It left me insufficient time to get into a hotel for a night's rest and be able to return for my morning flight.

I had been in the Chicago airport a number of times in my flights with Mary for my P's and Q's and knew of its extensive new addition added a few years before. It was a long walk from one end to another. My morning flight, wouldn't you know, was slated to leave from one of the new extensions.

At eighty-seven, my only option seemed to be to spend the night stretched out on a park bench halfway down a connecting hallway. The only other folk I saw were members of the wee small morning-hours cleaning crew. Wow, what huge equipment they dragged around!

Remembering this adventure, I recall thinking of my son, David, and the cell phone he gave me in case I ever needed him. "Sorry, dear. It was of no value to me at that point. But thank you anyway. It was too far for you to drive."

I had no sense of trouble back then. It was all part of my adventure into cyberspace to locate a man to spend the rest of my life with. I would never again be lonely.

And my search had brought me what I sought. Clayton was a dream man. I knew my family would embrace him in disbelief and love. They would be so thankful for me and proud of what I had done. No, sleeping on a bench four years ago was nothing. I was walking on the moon, not sleeping on a wooden bench in an airport. I remember it all so well.

18

Railroading

The end of February, I found myself in the midst of planning a trip to Chicago to attend the Women on Fire convention. Winters are long where I live, full of snow and cold. There were years when I was in heaven over this, back when I was a skier.

Once one celebrates their eightieth birthday, those about you begin to tell you to stay inside and off the darn slippery snow. I ignored this as often as I could, but Ed and I did have limits, and winters began to stretch out longer and longer with no outdoor activities available.

Normally I would not get the least bit excited about attending a women's convention; I've just never had interest in such festivals. But without skiing to keep me active in the wintertime, I was ready to get out and do almost anything.

The national group, Women on Fire, I'd met with in Traverse City the previous fall at a tea. They were convening a larger area annual meeting beginning on a Friday evening and ending on Sunday morning. Most of its attendees would be women much younger than me and in the working world.

I decided to go. Remembering the wonderful Hollywood movie producer I had met in the fall, I had a different outlook on the gathering. Because weather seemed to thwart my recent air travel, I made my plans to arrive by train.

The railroad terminal was in downtown Chicago about four blocks from the hotel the meetings would be held in. The airport was out of town, down on the southwestern side. Even if I had to grab a taxi, it would be far less expensive. I'd drive south two hours to Grand Rapids to catch the train. My car could be safely left in its Michigan parking lot.

So I found myself arriving in late March. Much to my amazement, the national leader and creator of Women on Fire, Debbie Phillips, remembered me. I realized it wasn't me who was memorable but rather my ancient age. It simply fascinated other women an almost ninety-year-old woman was out, about and active. I guess they believed all women my age were tucked away in rest homes, staring at the walls or sound asleep. Heck, it fascinated me, too!

Before I left, I contacted Don, a new man I'd been online with for a few weeks, to see if we could say hello somehow while I was there. This had nothing to do with Clayton. Rather I saw it as an opportunity to reach out to a man whose wife was nearing the end of her siege with Alzheimer's disease and encourage him to find another woman after her death.

Having undergone the long battle with my Ed and knowing society's tendency to look down its nose at such behavior by the healthy spouse, I wanted to encourage him to continue his search. I pointed out the process of finding another woman online to love took time. And once located, she would understand getting together would have to be after death.

I had explained all this to Clayton and he understood. He was even proud of me and joked about it.

Don was a retired attorney living on the fifteenth floor of a large condo overlooking Lake Michigan in downtown Chicago. Once his two sons finished college, his wife had walked out on him because of his increased drinking. He was so hurt by her decision he bounced right off the stuff in his effort to reclaim her. She didn't trust him. Because she failed to return, he eventually had found another woman and had been with her twenty years.

Although no marriage had occurred, he had remained faithful to her. Oh, you are thinking, "Why is he online?" Doesn't sound faithful to me. She had been diagnosed two years earlier with Alzheimer's. Although she couldn't help it, Don told me it felt to him like she was leaving him, too. The thought of living without a woman at his side just wasn't something he wanted. He was preparing to solve the problem. I understood he had no timeline. That remained out of his hand.

If you have been directly involved with an Alzheimer's victim, you would understand. It is normally a lengthy illness. Ed's lasted eight diagnosed years. I have no idea how long he was under its touch before we first visited the doctor. It often progresses slowly, transforming the partner's life into a time of dread, nothing but watching it all happen.

One's mind automatically begins to ponder the years ahead. For me, I had Ed's request for me to go on living with another. I am certain these feelings caused Don to go online. Wondering what it would be like to once again have a companion after his love died, or would it even be possible at his age? He confessed his true circumstances in his second letter to me. I assured him I understood and saw nothing wrong in looking forward to his life on down the road. He thanked me.

Then Don assured me he would not leave his woman until she was no longer capable of knowing who he was. At that point, her daughter and husband with whom he was very close told him they wanted him to go on with his life. They would place her in a care center close to their home. He was to go back to a normal life. I found this amazing and unusually supportive.

Our e-mails were primarily about things he was doing in the meantime as a retiree within his profession and what she was doing. I was an online friend. Despite the doctor's warning, she refused to stop roaming about the city's enormous and busy center. She had been a psychiatric doctor.

Late that summer after our meet during the women's retreat, she climbed onto a city bus to return home from shopping and missed her stop. She found herself still on board when the bus reached the end of its run. Fortunately, the conductor was able to reach Don on her cell phone and make arrangements to return her. Don was there to meet her.

Within a week of this happening, the family arrived to help Don pack her for the trip back with them. He told me what an awful time they all had, but once settled, she seemed happier. He was moving into a smaller one-bedroom apartment in the same building.

Don's apartment was relatively close to the gathering's hotel, and we were able to officially meet at lunch. We had seen each other in photos online, but it is so different to actually clasp the other's hand and say hello.

It was good being together after all our weeks online. Don agreed he would like to repeat our time the next day while I was still in Chicago.

The following lunch hour, he arrived on his bike. He was an ardent believer in physical activities for those in their late eighties. He played golf and even participated in weekly gymnastics! I had to admire him for that. But that didn't change my mind when arriving back at my room after the luncheon he asked if he could enter with me and stay a bit longer.

Of course, I refused. "Don," I said, "you promised yourself to remain faithful to your wife as long as she was still living."

I don't think he was surprised at my refusal, but I suppose like any seven-second man, Don thought it worth trying.

I was glad I had decided to make it down to the women's meeting and have the opportunity to meet Don. Through our brief time of letter writing, I created an image of him in my mind. That image turned out to be right on the money.

Clayton called the evening I returned home. I had told him of my meeting. I thought he might ask me some questions about my time in Chicago and bring up the how and when of our wedding. But he didn't ask any questions about my journey or the wedding because he had some worries of his own. He was extremely despondent over some bad news regarding his international brokerage firm.

On top of being a Methodist pastor, a university professor, and psychiatrist, Clayton had developed his side business. With two partners who each lived miles away in Massachusetts and Oklahoma, he bought and sold exchange items such as coal, grain, diamonds, and gold internationally. When we first met, he proudly told me of his successes and of one trip all the way to Australia. The current deal which had hit a big problem would have netted him and his partners over three million dollars.

But Clayton discovered the seller had lied. He told me, "Anne, the guy who said he had the product we finally sold confessed that it was no longer his. In all my years in this business, I have never run into anyone like him."

I heard the disappointment in his voice at the loss and the realization such a dishonest person existed.

I saw nothing in the problem I should worry about. Oh, I understood it was a huge disappointment. His business was a wonderful way for him to use his spare time. He so loved sharing the huge sums of money with his theological college. In my mind, Clayton's money was his to do with as he pleased. I was proud of him for giving it away as he had.

I knew he had no millions tucked in his back pocket. He had told me my airline ticket was purchased from the Christmas bonus the church had given him. Money was not what I was online searching for. It had never entered my mind. After all, if I managed to exist on my social security check, certainly we could do even better if we put ours together.

19

What a Price

This whole thing about money seamed to rear its head all the time. It certainly did with another man I had tried repeatedly to brush off for some time. He was a seventy-year-old man in Florida, George Charles. He kept coming back to tell me I was beautiful and he was deeply in love. He desperately wanted to wrap me in his arms and all the other passionate words his mind found to dish out.

Somehow I could find nothing interesting in a man young enough to be a son of mine. No, I knew my man should be my age or even a bit older. Only then could we look at the world about us with the same eyes. So I pointed out my thinking to George. Yes, that was his name. Beside the age bit, there were the miles between us and over and over they had reared their ugly head up between the men I wrote.

After a few days, I gave up and went online with him again to point out our age difference. He would be like a son to me plus the many miles between us. Then I wished him good luck online and good-bye.

He ignored my farewell. His letter explained age was only a man-made thing and had absolutely nothing to do with love. And as far as the miles between us, they would disappear as soon as he completed his current contract. He was an electronic contractor. I would be in his arms, etc., etc.

George then wrote. "My wife was older than me and died five years back. I am desperate to have a woman to love and couldn't wait to get up to you and hold you, etc., etc. Will you go on chat with me and send me your phone number so we can talk?'

Another Will?

I simply wasn't interested in getting involved with another man. The man I loved so deeply would be with me in the near future.

No, my tomorrows were off in the future somewhere. My mind was not communicating with me in its usual way. It ignored me because somehow I sent Mr. Florida my phone number. When it rang, I couldn't believe what I had done. I wondered what it was about him that led me to do something I didn't really want to.

When I heard George's voice, I had a terrible time understanding him. He explained this to me. "I was born in Finland, moved to England, and once I married, my wife wanted to come over to the US to live. Our only son is still in England attending college. I'm alone."

Somehow his explanation didn't make sense to me. His accent wasn't what I thought was Finnish or British. It was too weird. His answer was he would go on chat with me, not use the phone.

I received musical cards, calls to join him on chat, etc. It was all giving me something to shake my head over and mumble about during those days of waiting.

His excited voice explained after midnight the previous night a large firm in Cairo, Egypt, had hired him via e-mail to do electronic installation for them. George had been negotiating with them for some time. I could hear the excitement in his voice.

It was then I understood he was in Egypt. He had flown over during the night thanks to a six-hour time difference. He had a local man who spoke English who was assigned to him as an assistant. He was staying in his apartment.

I could hear the excitement in his voice. Obviously this was to be a huge financial contract. He was about to leave to meet with those who had hired him. I wished him a wonderful day. It was the same day, in the evening, when another call arrived. I couldn't make out what he was trying to tell me. I could tell it was something else unexpected. I asked him to e-mail me. The e-mail arrived. He was terribly upset.

The company would not allow him to order the electronics needed for installation. They were not to be charged to the company but were to be purchased by him. He hadn't gone over to Egypt prepared to have to furnish the equipment. This had never been pulled on him before.

In sympathy, I asked how much. He replied, "Four thousand dollars."

My father was a construction contractor and had always supplied all his materials. But that was residential, not commercial building. I said, "Well, you got yourself over there in less than twenty-four hours. You should be able have your Florida bank express $4,000 to you just as fast."

George answered, "I've already spoken to them, and they couldn't send any of my money to me because of income tax the government wouldn't receive."

Then he asked, "Do you have some you could loan me? As soon as I am finished here, I could have it right back to you?"

My answer was, "Oh, I don't have that kind of money. I live on my social security check, and by the end of a month, I seldom have any left. No, you have to talk to your friends for your needs. My gosh, we have never even met! I can tell you are desperate and upset. If the bank can't help you, try your car dealer—maybe he will swap your car there in Florida for the money you must have."

In response, George told me he had tried it all. No luck.

"If you don't have the large sum, could you scrape up $500 so I can buy food?

I responded, "I don't have even that to help you out. The best I can do is $25." I told him I would get to the bank and see if I had it. With that, I hung up.

Leaning back in my chair, I waited for my mind to catch up with all it had just heard. Not once in the unbelievable number of men I had corresponded with did even one ever ask me for money. It is just not the natural makeup of a man to lean on a woman for money. Especially one they are just meeting and getting to know. No, it had never happened. In fact, I found the opposite true.

When something they yearned for involved my spending money, they had handed me what was needed. Not as a loan but a gift. Thus, Leighton had sent me the money for my plane trip down to be in his arms.

No, George who claimed his love for me was beyond all his words wasn't after my love but my money.

He had envisioned me as a wealthy old bag, not a beautiful woman to love. He was a con artist, and I was his intended victim. After all my time online, I had finally met a con artist—my only one. Society claims they infest cyberspace in frequent numbers. Not so.

I became excited. I wanted to be able to teach this man a lesson about us old women. We are not brainless. I took myself to the bank and withdrew $25 to send to Egypt. I wanted to ride his con journey with him as far as I could afford. I wanted to teach him. I looked at my $25 as a reasonable investment if it would save others from him.

Even the woman at the 'send money' station tried her best to stop me from sending the $25 although I lied and said, "I know the man I am sending it to."

She told me one horror story after another. And having spent the time I had with George Charles, I could understand how these intelligent, unimaginable liars manage to rake in other person's money.

I sent the money looking at it as an investment in my online search I was endeavoring for a lover. I wanted so to prove the public attitude about it as way off base. And I knew by then I was thinking correctly. The public was just talking about something they had next to no knowledge about. I wanted to share this unbelievably gifted man with others.

It didn't excite him. Yet obviously he still believed me to be one of his "victims." It was not returned to me. I called my grandson, Pat, to tell him what I was up to. Much like the women at the money country counter, he urged me not to ever send anymore. "Grandma, men like him are professionals. Be careful."

I reassured him, "My plan is to absolutely not be taken. I just want to stay connected to learn what other procedures he has tucked away to try on me."

Four or five days passed with just the usual love talk and "free" musical cards. Then another request arrived for me to help him get the $4,000 he needed so badly. He had finally made contact with another Florida contractor. He was a friend and they often shared problems. The friend was going to send George the money as soon as George worked out a legitimate way to get it. Edward's answer involved me. "My love, will you send me your bank account number? I will share it with my friend, and he will send the money I need to your account. When it arrives, you can send it on to me. Is that okay? Will you get me your account number?"

So, once the money arrived in my account, I was to withdraw it and send it to George via Western Union. I understood immediately once he had the bank number, he was planning to remove its entire contents and disappear from my world. He was so certain my account had wads of money in it. There was no such person as the friend in Florida to give him money. No, I was the money gal! Me.

I answered by telling him I had two bank accounts. One was a trust fund and the other a business account. I would run into the bank and see which one they would advise me to use. I suspected they would advice the business one. I told him this as I figured he would think it the one with the most money. I would e-mail him its name and password as soon as I got back home.

Once at the bank, I sought out its manager and told her my need and why. She shook her head firmly, "Anne, don't go any further with this guy."

I told her my reason, and she just shook her head but preceded to advice me. I described my idea. "If I open a new account to use with him, will he have no way to access what money I have? It is important to me to see where he plans to go with this latest effort to borrow money. He is so certain I am a wealthy old woman. With a new account, I won't have to worry about his getting the little money I do have. I'll just deposit $25 in this new one."

She assured me there was no bank charge to open an account, and any money in my other two accounts could not be accessed in any way through it. Understanding my thinking, she proceeded to open the new account for me.

On my return home, I e-mailed the new account information to Egypt. He responded with lots of love and a thank-you. I promised him I would alert him the minute the money arrived for me to forward on to him. Three days passed and no money arrived at the bank, just as I had thought. I e-mailed George to advice him of this.

His voice was despondent as he told me, "My friend for reasons no one could name has suddenly left the US and no one is able to contact him."

I smiled. I had been right in my surmise he had tried to set up a way to withdraw money from my bank. He envisioned it having at least $4,000. All he had found was the $25. In his disappointment he had not touched it. He was still viewing me as a rich, old retired bag. I had out conned a super con artist. My day was made.

I had come to believe neither his name nor profile photo were his. I had Goggled *George Charles* in his Florida city and discovered over thirty. It had been an excellent choice for him. I also suspected he was well under seventy, perhaps even in his twenties or thirties. His conversation fit that age group. I was 99 percent certain he lived in some country other than the United States and probably had a number of women online every day as he sought to steal their money. I suspected some of his unusually beautiful love statements were copies of work of known writers. I credited him with high intelligence.

In my "Good-bye" letter, I shamed him for his time consuming crooked lifestyle. I suggested at his age and with his brains now was the time to become a man who saw all others as those he should reach out to in helpful ways; for him to use his seven-second thinking to center on one woman and their life together. I never heard another word from him. I reported him to the service.

George was the only con artist out of over four hundred men I would correspond with in my trip among seniors online. Regular online men do not ask women for money—never, for any reason.

However, many men do believe the only reason a woman goes online to search for a man has nothing to do with her desire to have a lover but rather his money? Society has brainwashed them in this attitude. It has even brain washed daughters of online men.

So, if you are a wonderful online man who can't stand his loneliness, be frank about your money as well as to the woman with whom you are interested. You are both adults and can be honest and find a workable way to manage you expenditures. If you are with another, there might well be money. You have to do those things you wouldn't be able to alone. After all, you each worked years to have it to enjoy in your retirement.

20

The Dinner Table

When I consider the fact I exchanged letters with so many men online, I find myself shaking my head in denial. I admit the majority of them have slowly dripped out of my dome, but there are those who will never disappear. I find myself wishing them great health and wonderful mates.

One such man amazes me because he is so firmly tucked inside of me. We only exchanged my "Hello," his response, and my thank-you. His online name was SGstringer. He only lived thirteen miles farther away from me than Mr. NY. Of course, there was a matching reaction.

As I read Clarence's prologue, I found it difficult to believe a man alive had the ability to write as he did. I reread his words again and then, once again. They resonated within me. I had an immediate desire to spend time with the man to ascertain the things he wrote were true. His last words, "Laugh with all their laughter and cry with all their tears," echoed throughout me,

I said to myself, "Do your best for me on this one, will you?" I turned out an especially beautiful letter for him as my initial contact.

> Dear CG,
>
> Will you please explain to me why it is here at my computer off in the upper regions of Michigan I sit and read about you and all you are only to recognize you are my echo? What are we to do with the miles stretching between us?

We could write wondrous prose in all our years to come but what about the driving, growing need to share our love—the reawakened desire caged within us as we look down the years stretching out ahead? Our generation is desperately seeking a venue allowing us to re-mate and continue living. Yet being online is not proving to be the avenue—the miles separating only increase our frustration.

We seem to be the first generation to hit this stone wall. Those before us, once widowed or separated merely pulled up a comfortable chair to sit it out, accepting the fact the joys, sorrows, love, and glorious feelings of being alive were only to be found in their world of memories. Yet all those generations lined up ahead us will come more and more to accept our outlook. We need to fix the system. We must conquer the distances. How do we manage to meet each other? You in NY and me in MI?

Your eyes, fantastic smiles, words, and honesty about who you are and what you desire, the way you embrace life and so candidly speak of your physical needs so reached me. Please read my profile. I too am a writer and an artist (the latter was my college degree; the first my passion). I have a third book in the first draft stage and am excited about it. I love music but do not have the gift of voice. I treasure stage performances and am in my twelfth year designing and painting sets—although I am not allowed to use a scaffold anymore. People who know my age expect me to be cautious. I realize this is wise but so hard for me to accept. I was a college prof one semester long ago at the University of Southern California in Fresno. It was then at the age of twenty an amazing happening occurred to me.

Because my father was a home-builder, he had taught me at a very early age how to design a home. His instructions required my learning first to draw its structure from the foundation to the chimney top. While in college in California, *McCall's Magazine* with its New York City headquarters, opened a contest for a post-war home design. It could be traditional or modern and involved four sections—kitchen, living room, bedroom, and dining room. Thinking about the whole idea, I guessed the magazine was looking for a handsome service man and his wife to win the modern home division. My guess was on the money. The $25,000 first prize I won was like a million today!

I lost my one-in-a-million husband last January to a long illness of a type of physical Alzheimer's—in which his wonderful body was affected, not so much his mind. We were married sixty-five years, and I do believe in love at first sight—I was a WWII bride.

There are trains, buses, cars, planes, garden tractors, and skateboards—and wondrous places between to meet and share some time. But if I suggest such a thing, I am being unwomanly and far too aggressive—so as a creative man, what are your thoughts? Do we just write and continue to tantalize each other for a few weeks or months as we age further—or do we talk on the phone or chat? What are your thoughts? Or are you content to just talk about your hopes and dreams? You see, I am very interested in you. Certainly as a friend and perhaps more (whoops, I don't meet your criteria—but I really do—those who meet me consider me about sixty-five or seventy years of age—I love it!).

Anne

Within minutes, CGstringer's reply arrived. Not what I hoped for, but in many ways one of the most insightful correspondence I had enjoyed since starting forth on my adventure.

Dear Anne,

Thank you so much for the thoughtful e-mail. It was honest and revealing and interesting. It does seem that we have much in common. However, there are a couple of major problems. As you rightly acknowledge distance is considerable. I'm not much into chatting on the phone. In fact I usually have my phone turned off. My roots here are very deep. I live in a house that's 275 years old. It sort of enfolds me. My family is here. Finally, just recently, via "Match" I've met someone in the neighboring village. So far, the relationship is going quite well, but it's just beginning. You are a fine writer. I'm sure the books will be successful. You're a fine woman. I'm sure your search will be equally successful.

Reading your profile and e-mail reminds me of a piece I used as an introduction to my writing classes. I'll add it here.

The Feast

There is a poem by Victor Hugo ends with these words, "I'll soon leave in the middle of the feast, but the world will lose nothing of its size of glory." I think that's mostly true, but it may not be the whole truth. What matters is the feast. We have all been invited. A few, in their ignorance refuse the invitation. Others, in their ignorance, get up in the middle of the feast. They go to the porch for a cigarette and never come back. They hang out in the rest room and never return.

Most, however, remain at the festive table. Their lives are rich with life's joys and life's sorrows. They "laugh with all their laughter and cry with all their tears." To be at the fest is to experience life fully. When it is their turn to turn down an empty glass and go on their solitary way, they do so graciously and give thanks for having been invited.

Some of the guests try to capture special moments, make an attempt to preserve those moments, both large and small when they were truly alive, intensely aware, passionately involved. In these efforts they preserve, if not the feast itself, at least its memory. They leave evidence that they were in attendance, and that they, indeed, attended. Writing does this for me. It helps me attend. It makes me sharply aware of the feast. It records, however, inadequately the wonder of it.

It reminds me of a fine book which was made into an equally fine movie called *Zorba the Greek*. At one point, Zorba, a huge man of passionate feelings and great appetites, is seasick on a small crowded steamer crossing the Aegean Sea. Clutching the ship's rail, sweating profusely, and throwing up the last of his lunch, he suddenly sees a trio of dolphins, rising in graceful arcs alongside the ship. Forgetting his distress, Zorba points to the dolphins and calls out to the others, "Look. Look."

For me there is always, it seems, just behind my right ear, a small Zorba-like figure pointing and shouting, "Look. Look." But talk is not enough. The unexpected act is not fully experienced. Life equals experience. To complete an experience, we must find a way to express it. The special moments we experience at the festive table may be expressed in a variety of ways—music, sculpture, painting, dance, writing. I find and I hope you will too, to write it down, to put words to the pain and joy of life's enriches, and in some minor way perpetuate those moments when I sat at the festive table.

The feast is temporary. That we know. Age, infirmity, and death are landlords who, before we are quite ready to leave, usher us out. And with the quiet closing of the door behind us, "the world loses nothing of its size or glory." But the words I put down will have helped me realize the splendor of it all. And if by chance those words turn out to be wonderful words, they will have added some small measure to its size and glory.

I think you are very much at the feast. Yes?

Namaste,
Chuck

Once again, a possible online friendship came to an abrupt closure.

At least it wasn't a slammed door. I felt honest disappointment as I would have enjoyed continuing our conversation about the power of words for an extended time. But obviously this was a man who was involved deeply with his family, work, home, and life. A man who had decided he had no room in his life for yet another friend as far away as Michigan. Despite all his intelligence and knowledge in the world of words, Chuck was failing to realize love is the commodity which never diminishes and only becomes stagnate when one limits the sharing of it. Who can ever have too many friends in this wonderful world God has given mankind?

21

Love's Way

Sitting here and thinking back to the spring and summer of my second year online, I am surprised I stuck to it. It had begun as I became happily engaged to Clayton, an unbelievably wonderful man. Even my family expressed their interest in him. They were anxiously waiting to meet him when he would arrive in June. They had never dreamed I would come up with a minister!

I had accomplished what I set out to do.

The further I moved into cyberspace, the deeper my understanding of it became.

At first I didn't find myself concocting elaborate wedding plans. I somehow understood Clayton would desire just a quiet marriage at my church, perhaps with family. We would ask my son-in-law, Paul, to officiate at his church in Cadillac about one hundred miles south of Boyne. Then we would return to North Carolina to take up our lives in the apartment he was seeking. I was in a state of bliss hard to accept—it was so dreamlike. Yet I knew how true it was. My heart was with Clayton and his with me.

Clayton's calls came every evening. We always had something to talk about. Yet as both April and May sauntered by he never once mentioned plans for June. I began to wonder if I should bring it up. Oh, he was the same Clayton as always. He always had something to tell me in his calls and questions to ask. We always shared laughter.

His brokerage company had definitely lost its big chance of selling, and as a result, the man out west had retired from the business, leaving only Clayton and his friend up East. The next thing he was telling me was the Eastern man had written to say he was in the hospital and wouldn't be able to help Clayton with anything for a while.

As if this wasn't enough, Clayton found it necessary to have his heart checked at the Veterans Hospital where he served as its chaplain. He didn't have to stay yet was put on some new medicine. I just couldn't find any way to bring up our marriage plans until he pulled himself out of all his problems. Because of his medical studies, I understood he would be aware of exactly what was going on with his body. He would work it all out.

Looking back, I realize how wrong I was. Having something positive and exciting to think about rather than his failures and those of his friends of so many years might have helped him get through it all easier. I should have brought it up, I know that now, but at the time I simply didn't know how. In those days, women didn't butt into their man's thinking. We didn't offer to advise them about decisions needing to be made. No, we let them find the answers they viewed as the best available. Ed's and my life had been lived in this manner. I never got over seeing him as the "captain" he was during WWII. His decisions had been the ones used.

All our years of marriage not once did I consider his answers anything but excellent. So it would be with Clayton.

June came and went. Clayton never mentioned our wedding plans. His calls never wavered. They arrived every night. It was as if we were already a married couple which habitually ended our days with each other, even though it was merely on the telephone.

In August, his younger daughter, then in her mid-thirties and her boyfriend of ten years, set their wedding date. Clayton was able to escort his daughter down the aisle there in his hometown. The trip turned into a time of laughter for him as he forgot to wear his belt. His pants barely stayed on as with his daughter he slowly made their way up to the pastor.

Despite all his chatter about this affair, he never once said a word about our wedding, which he had been so excited about the preceding spring. I drove down to Cadillac to talk to Nancy about all this.

She agreed with me. "Anne, I think it is his illness more than anything else. Remember he is a doctor. He understands whatever it is that is throwing him in and out of the hospital. He has given up on ever living long enough to marry you at this point."

"But," I interrupted. "Would it help him get through these 'end of time' days if I were down there beside him, even without marriage?" I could do things for him."

"No, Hon. I don't think it would. He has had such a mixed-up life I think he deserves and needs this time by himself. I believe his times on the phone with you every evening are exactly what he cherishes doing. I'm so sorry you are going through this. You don't deserve it."

By late fall, he was in and out of the hospital, week after week.

I find no answer as to why I simply didn't say, "Oh, by the way, Clayton, don't you think we need to talk about our wedding plans?" Something in me had concluded Clayton, in the silent way men manage to come to major decisions, had done so. He was among other things a medical doctor. He understood he was leaving his world.

My husband had done this twice to me. The first was when he reenlisted in the service to end up on Guam and the second was when he made the decision to leave Ohio and move up into Michigan. The difference was Ed included me once the decisions were made.

I believe Clayton's loss of his huge income affected his desire to buy the wonderful condo we had so liked. Then, looking down the road, he had seen his impending death way too soon for him to embark on a sixth marriage.

Also, he may have thought since I was a woman, he needed to have some big money to keep me happy. Oh, I know this is true of some women, but not all of us, please. It is especially not so when a woman is in her late eighties. By then you have had or done almost everything you really considered wonderful. It is companionship we are seeking, not big adventures. What I desired was to have my man's arms wrapped around me, not what he had in his pockets.

I suspect his basic monthly income was his social security check as mine was. He may have enjoyed a bit from his career but that is just a guess. I've since discovered men simply refuse to discuss money with women they meet online. I am certain society has brainwashed them about all women being conniving!

However, almost every man I corresponded with by his second letter told me he had prostate problems, if he had. This seemed the primary factor with each. None seemed to understand women have the desire to be with a man for his love, not just sex. After all, for centuries, this was the reason men have sought a mate. Oh, there was love, too. Yet intercourse is the way they needed to express it.

In the same manner, I was upfront about the money matter. The theory I presented was the cost of living together should be broken into two equal amounts, each contributing the money to pay one of the halves. What is left over belongs to its owner and his or her family.

There are times when the offspring don't stop to consider all the hours their parents have worked to enable themselves to have "savings" and dreams about what adventures they hope to enjoy with it before death interrupts. Advertisements tempt we ancient ones with trips, schools, sports events, museums, and concert halls we hunger to see and enjoy. But we don't want to do it alone. No, we plan to do this with our mates. When a mate passes away too soon, the desires remain.

Today's older lone people can search online for someone to do it with. Unlike me, many have the money in their savings to be able to afford such dreams.

I found this desire in all the men I corresponded with online. I came to believe if a partner can be found, the two should enjoy traveling together and whatever else interests them by using some of their hard-earned money tucked away in their savings. These longer lives need this despite tradition.

So I came to accept the fact Clayton's love for me was preventing him from allowing me to marry a man about to die. A couple of times I suggested to him that I would love to go down and be with him while he was hospitalized, but he wouldn't hear of it. Although disappointed and not in agreement, I didn't add to his troubles with an argument. I accepted his thinking with my love.

We remained together in love, thought and prayer. I talked to him on the telephone the evening before his death. I told him I was there beside him. His answer? "I know, my love." I suspected he didn't have the necessary money needed for my traveling and he would never dream of my paying my own way.

Clayton left on June 17, 2011, the day before our granddaughter, Rachael, married her fantastic Rutt. He was from Thailand, and they had met at Alma College. That same day my brother, David, died of cancer in Perrysburg, Ohio. As he had not shared his illness with any of the family, it was an unbelievable shock.

22

Prostrate Research

I remember all too well the changes in my attitude about online dating with the arrival of fall in 2010. Looking back, I all but feel the discouragement which held me in its grasp. Every high point in those sixteen months, all the exciting moments over the wonderful men I had met and who had reached out to me, even with marriage proposals, had all evaporated.

By the time September started predicting the coming of fall, the schools had reopened and the number of vacationers on the streets of my beloved little town diminished. I found myself in a discouraging world. With only Will and Don, I could see the months ahead as being anything from what I had come so close to experiencing. My daily online time seemed more a ritual than the adventure it had the year before. Oh, I understood my online chats, e-mails, and phone calls were keeping me from being lonesome. I looked forward to each.

In late September as the leaves began their annual show of unbelievable vivid colors, one profile caught my eye as I clicked on to my day's new "knocks." I can close my eyes and see it yet today. There stood a man next to a large painting, elbow braced against the wall next to it. Pride flooded his face and eyes. I knew instantly he was crazy about his painting. It appeared as if it might easily be by the well-known Mexican artist, Diego Rivera.

My first thought was to question him. "Is the painting your work?"

I sent off one of my "Have seen your profile and would appreciate exchanging letters with you." I inquired about the painting. Its reply told me I had met a very interesting man.

Dear Anne.

I wish my answer could be yes, but the painting was done by a longtime friend of mine. I treasure it. You sound interesting and it is my hope we can get to know each other much better. As you read in my profile, I have been the director of the college of medicine in both a large Texas and southern California University before entering anatomy research as the director of one of our country's eight research stations. I have found the work fascinating and although retired and eighty-four am currently teaching an eighteen-month series here in my retirement center, Gregorian Plaza in the near heart of Tacoma, Washington. My class of about sixty residents meets with me for two hours every other week. I am centering the study on the mind.

Please write and tell me more about yourself. I think we may be a great match.

Warm regards,
Vic

His letter was not only about the painting which he professed loving. It was all about him. But most exciting was his closing wish about wanting to know me better.

I so wanted to surge ahead with Vic, but after all my experiences online, I could only tell myself not to get too excited. After all, he was three years younger than me. Even more importantly, he was farther away from me than Mr. NYC's 639 miles. Checking out Tacoma on my atlas I discovered the distance was 2,600 miles. Despite all this, for the first time in weeks, I felt a deep desire to try once again to spend my lonely life with someone I could enjoy and do for.

Before I could push myself forward, Vic sent another letter in which he regretted the distance between us as he found me so interesting and attractive, but he had made a lunch date with one of the home's women for the following day. He hoped it would be a positive experience as he desperately wanted to do away with his lonely life, too.

I responded by wishing him a wonderful time and would he let me know how things turned out. He assured me he would.

Short notes arrived as one after another the woman cancelled their dates for unimportant woman reasons such as a hair appointment. Finally he simply gave it all up. His loneliness and discouragement overwhelmed me. Yet I knew nothing to do to encourage him. I did write a short note asking about the photograph of the large sail boat in his profile picture.

He said he had been an avid participant in the annual boat races between Oregon and Canada. His boat had required a crew of six, and they fought many angry seas as the race was in the early springs.

He asked that we exchange our personal e-mails as he felt it was so much simpler to correspond that way than through the dating site. This reminded me of Will's similar request and I agreed happily. Yet within minutes, a "second half" e-mail arrives in which he returned to his concerns about the distance between us. He didn't want to pursue our friendship only to have to hurt me. We might meet and things wouldn't be as he thought they would be. He wished me his deep affection and for success in my search.

Eight days had transpired and there I was seated at my computer hearing its door slam once more in my face. This thing among men about using mileage as a means not to move forward in their lonely lives made absolutely no sense to me.

My anger roared the more I thought about the various times this had hit me in the face from the very start. I even discovered I held a deep anger with Clayton for his kind, gentleman-like manner in which he alone, without any discussion with me, and what I might think, had set me aside as he proceeded to travel to his death. It wasn't fair!

I turned back to the computer. Using his personal e-mail address, I wrote Vic, asking him to telephone me as soon as it was convenient. He did within a couple hours.

Our conversation was long, yet in the very beginning, we agreed with our ages under consideration we should not wait months to meet. It would be only when standing face to face we would understand where our feelings were in regard to the other.

We shared stories of things we had learned during our marriages and lives which were affecting our thinking and the depth of our needs. He explained he had had prostate issues. But he harbored hope he might have a way to repair his problem. That he needed to apply experimental meds in the privacy of his apartment with the assistance of a person who understood his need. Was I willing to do so?

With my lifelong interest in medicine, I assured him I would do all I could to help. I had more than once in my thirties helped my brother as his chair nurse when his regular nurse was absent.

At that moment, Vic surprised me by suddenly asking me to marry him if all went well at our meet. My reaction was not one of utter, speechless surprise as it had been with Clayton, but rather deep happiness.

So it was we made plans for me to arrange my flights, select the times and he would send me a check to cover the costs. When it arrived, it had an additional $100 tucked in, for snacks and so forth. So it was I flew westward on October 3 to return on the twentieth.

I was excited and optimistic as I climbed on board the plane at the Traverse City airport. It was the same starting point for my trip down to meet Clayton the year before, and, yes, Sue Ellen helped me get on the plane.

Thanks to the time difference my plane arrived ten thirty-seven the same morning. Yet I was airborne six and a half hours. Once there, I had to get my luggage out to the taxis. Vic had warned me of his knee problems. They were the result of a serious infection following knee surgery. He had to use a walker so couldn't take on the long passages and hallways one has to negotiate to leave a terminal. I understood.

Once at the humongous retirement center in the heart of the city, I registered as a guest and was given instructions of how to take the elevator and locate Vic's apartment on the twelfth floor. There were fifteen in all. He was waiting at his door, ready with a big hug and kiss!

I am certain neither of us were even slightly disappointed in the other. Once he had tucked away all my gear and shown me the wheres and hows of his domain, we sat down with lunch. He had brought it up from the center's café. We started talking in our eagerness to know each other.

Our lives had been identical yet extremely different in many ways, too. But isn't this the way with all of us? Think about it, and if married, add the husband. We are all human beings and react to our lives in our own manner. In cyberspace, this becomes an expected fact as you open each letter. You wonder what a new man will be like, not who he is or what he does. What he was all his life is his story; it is where he is now in his retirement which is important. His past has created his world as surely as it has for others and mine for me.

Vic and I found each other as we surmised and enjoyed every minute. There was so much to learn and share that our conversation never lagged.

He even bent over to me and said, "What if we go to Hawaii on our honeymoon? I have found an engagement ring I really like and I hope you will feel for it too." All this carried on as we enjoyed the deli sandwiches. Later in the afternoon, he poured us wine as I sat within his arms on his comfy two-person couch to watch the evening news.

The salmon he prepared for dinner was great. He put things away afterward as I washed the dishes, not enough to bother with the dishwasher. As things began to slow down, Vic asked, "Would you enjoy watching a couple of films I rented which deal with intercourse for the elderly?" There it was again, the seven-second world of men.

Considering his background as a college professor in medical courses and research, I suspected the film would not be pornography but rather scientific scenes from some research program. I was on the money!

I commented to Vic, "These films divulge nothing new to anyone our ages. They must have been created for those younger in years."

He agreed. I suspected Vic, like so many, believed women lost interest in sex as part of their lives as they aged. Someone my age may have forgotten it entirely! It was so obvious he was endeavoring to bring me back into his world of sex.

I sat and listened to that brilliant man and felt sorry for him and his thoughts. I remembered in one of his earlier letters he had asked me if I masturbated. I told him I didn't do that. I wasn't interested in being my own lover. I had experienced wonderful loving from my husband, Ed. Nothing else could hold a candle to the real thing. I believe we are all put together in that way.

Vic's effort to understand my opinion about sex was so obvious. He had no idea I was sitting there silently laughing in memory of my brother Doc's seven second theory. For someone like me who had gone through so many diverse traumas in my lifetime, it had become a huge waste of time to sit and worry about a bunch of what-ifs. Life simply takes charge and does as it must despite our carefully executed plans to do something entirely different.

In contrast to my attitude about my tomorrows, Vic obviously looked ahead and charted his course. His way was methodical and carefully thought out. When things went wrong, it must have been terribly painful. I hoped I could cheer up his tomorrows. I knew just being with him promised me tomorrows beyond my most fantastic dreams. I had not foreseen a man like Vic as part of my life.

He was a very handsome man despite his age. And as we began our time together, I found him so energetic I forgot he was using a walker. And like me, when he looked back on his long life, he saw how that which had been painful had in the end been beneficial. He wasn't overly proud of what he had accomplished but rather thankful he had had the opportunity to accomplish it. He saw the positive in others and understood their failures. He wasn't critical of others but understanding.

I even appreciated the fact he wore everyday jeans and T-shirts rather than his professional suits. Most of all his love of the outdoors was wonderful for me. All the things he promised me we would do he carried out to the very smallest detail. He drove me all over the state from the ocean to the mountains. I could tell that he, like me, treasured it all.

Once we were both ready for bed, he brought from the refrigerator a small black leather case holding the medicines he had written me about. Seated on the edge of his bed (it was to be my bed; he was using the fold-away cot) beside me, he unzipped it to display two small but full bottles plus one empty one. He also extracted a syringe and disinfectant tissues.

Because of my fascination with all that was medical, I was actually entranced as Vic poured the contents of both bottles into the third. He then screwed its lid on and shook it methodically. Inserting the syringe, he filled it with the clear liquid he had created.

Much to my surprise, he handed me the instrument carefully explaining what I was to do. "Insert this needle into the base of my penis as I hold him up."

Reaching into his PJ bottoms, he produced his tiny sleeping penis and endeavored to stretch it upward as far as possible. Nodding his head, he indicated the exact spot I was to aim for. I winced as I stabbed the poor thing. I was certain Vic must have felt it. He didn't say a word.

There was a momentary strengthening of the small appendage before it fell back to sleep. Vic proceeded to do a great job in accepting the failure of the medicine. No curse of disappointment or moan emerged from him. Silently and systematically, he gathered his meds, tossing the remaining in their zippered case. He then proceeded out of the bedroom to secure them in the refrigerator.

I waited for him to return. I so wanted to commiserate with him over the failure of such a great medical idea.

On his return, there was no discussion of the experiment's failure. Before I could say a word he came back to sit on the edge of the bed. Looking at me seriously he asked, "Anne I asked you online if you masturbated and you replied, 'no'. But in today's world where prostate is such a large problem I think you should understand how to give yourself a thrill. I will demonstrate the 'how' of it for you."

Reaching over, he pulled my nightgown up to my waist and then placed his fingers between my legs and proceeded to give me my lesson. We were both almost hysterical before he decided I knew how to perform the act and withdrew his fingers.

He held out his arms, gave me a big hug and kiss, and said, "You are an excellent student." His laughter filled the room as he turned and crawled into the foldaway.

The lights were turned off. Not another word was said. I turned over in my bed, wondering if I was just a part of yet another scientific research project for the brainy gent. He certainly had set the stage for tonight's experiment with his experimental drugs and hope for a return to active sex.

I thought, "Does this man have questions about the sexual desires of ancient women like me?" I suspected right there he could very well have. I knew of no other research in the field except for the time I discovered it in the Kansas College in my before online venture, "Remember the professor who sought information on how many persons in their eighties were actively engaged in sex."

Was it possible Vic, like most men I'd met online near or at my age, had decided the normal functioning of the penis is a must for any woman they might reach out to? Have they not learned we women do not think of sex when we meet a man but rather his personality? Prostate problems as they are pictured on TV today remain strictly from a masculine viewpoint in my mind's eye.

I had no idea how to ease Vic's mind on the subject of sex between the two of us once he placed the ring he had seen on my finger. But I was certain two people like us who had such a hunger for many more years of happy living would have no problem finding a great answer.

Looking back, I realize I did to Vic exactly the same thing I have accused Clayton, Will, and other online men of doing to me. I did not discuss our problems with him to give us an opportunity to solve them. I kept all my thoughts, suspicions, and possible answers to myself. I will always wonder why I was so silent. If I had spoken up, what might have been the results? The life with another I so determinedly was searching for? But, no, I remind myself. You knew you were doing exactly what your generation was taught to do and expect to do. You were taught women did not question men.

23

Amazing Man

I can still taste the breakfast Vic set out in front of me on the table the next morning. It was oatmeal with fresh strawberries cooked in it—delicious! As we drank our coffee, we answered a series of questions we had about each other, our lives, and our families.

The dining room was merely a partial addition of the small living room at its one end. Its table was tucked near a wall cabinet which displayed dishes, magazines, and books. Another side of the area was open to his tiny kitchen. What saved all this tucked away area was the enormous view of the river and mountains down below the center. It was down in that area where I would run the track once a day while Vic took his swim time in the center's pool.

Vic had had four children as Ed and I did—two girls and two boys. However, our marriages had taken different courses. Instead of staying together as Ed and I had for sixty-five years, his wife had left him once their children were college graduates.

His wonderful position in research caused his income to rise. She had wanted to move into the elite neighborhood and join two ritzy golf clubs. But Vic had worn suits, shirts, and ties for years. He was ready to enjoy casual clothes all day long, no matter where he might be.

He had no desire to live his life socially. She chose to part from him. He said he had split his income with her at the time.

During the intervening years, he had tried out a couple other women but neither had proved to be for him. It had been twelve years. He'd found each passing year more difficult as he tried to find things to do to fill his days.

I realized I was hearing his side of the story only. Perhaps his wife told a different one. Yet I felt his was true for him.

I spoke about my late life. How Ed slowly left my world and I turned to writing for the first time in my long life. I wrote *The Book of Anne* about raising our grandchildren and published it. I told him about the promise Ed had extracted from me about finding a man to spend the last years of my life with.

Vic told me, "When I moved here to the park, my two boys helped me."

He then spoke of the wonderful benefits it offered in helping him with his leg problem. The swimming pool and exercise room plus the auditorium in which he gave his lectures all were part of their contributions.

At this point, he paused and said, "In fact, we should light out tomorrow to travel up into the Mt. Rainer country as I will have to be back for Thursday's class."

I assured him the sooner the better. I couldn't wait to roam about Washington, the only state I had never visited. Returning to our talk, he explained his financial situation, including his monthly income and investment savings. He assured me if he left first I would inherit his money as all his children were financially great.

I shared with him my income was only Social Security as I'd had to sell my home during the 2008 recession and that Ed and my savings disappeared as we parented our grandchildren. But I was managing, not endeavoring to remarry because of money. What was his belonged to his family and ditto for mine.

Vic praised me, "Anne, my dear, I know of no one else who has done what you have." I assured him we were the fortunate ones to have had such a second life to enjoy.

There was a shared feeling of having known each other for a long, long time. I was eighty-serve and he, eighty-five. I believe our age created this unbelievable state as we shared the world of living for decades. Each had lived in their own manner yet in an unbelievable sameness through the times of being children, then youth, college, World War II, marriage, the arrival of our families, failures, successes, pain, and joy.

Vic and I had ridden the same train on the same track. Yet we had stopped at different spots and viewed unlike landscapes through its windows. There we were together and enjoying every minute. It seemed a miracle yet at the same moment the most believable thing we could imagine.

As we cuddled on the couch with our wine and the TV ranting about the upcoming elections, I wondered what had happened to our trip to purchase the wedding ring he had been so excited about and plans to go to Hawaii. But being the woman I am, I didn't ask.

There was no reference to the past night's failed medical experiment. Not even as we planned to head out to travel, laugh, and grow closer. The feeling between us in our time together was of a brother and sister. There was no love mentioned and not a word about sex. The seven-second man of our e-mail and telephone days had disappeared.

I silently digested all this. I had no way to enter his mind to see what was going on in there. He was the mental expert. No, all my life I had never questioned another about the how or why they were doing what they were. I could only share my opinions when asked.

Once Vic and I were on our way traveling and we had to share a bed during our exploration of the beautiful country and mountainsides, he clung to one side of the bed and I to the opposite as far apart as possible. The use of the bathroom was always granted to me first. The occasional hugs and smooches were those one would share with a relative, not one's love.

Yes, eventually I acknowledged to myself something was hanging between us. As we bonded closer and closer, it seemed to increase. Vic had withdrawn from all his man talk with me. In no other manner did our time together disintegrate. Although he took me numerous places around his city, even to its outstanding and very large bookstore, he never mentioned the ring he so excitedly discussed on our first day together.

Our stay in a darling ocean side condo for three days was so great. It had a cozy pull-down wall bed, a real wood fireplace, plus a two-person dining table with a vase of roses. After dinner which we concocted together, we settled in on the front deck to watch a huge glistening orange sun sink into the ocean.

Turning to me, Vic asked, "Why don't you walk down to the water, honey? I would if I could, but with my leg, it is a no-no.

I responded, "Okay, I will. Bet in your earlier years you and your family were in that water as often as possible?" He nodded yes as I climbed down off the porch and headed shoreward.

The second day, Vic announced, "Come on, my dear. Let's go into a nearby village for dinner and see the ships at anchor in its harbor."

He was engrossed in the ships, and I was taken by the large number of enormous walruses who had draped themselves onto a huge wooden dock just below the platform we stood on. They were sleeping, moving about and ignoring all of us.

Vic let me have all the time I desired to paint a small picture of the harbor and walruses. A little girl and her mother came by to watch me. I handed the girl a piece of my drawing pad, a brush and access to the paints on my pallet as I looked at her mother, silently asking permission. As Vic and I enjoyed dinner at a nearby restaurant, he talked of his children, all grown adults—of their marriages, work, children, where they lived, and their hobbies. I talked the same path about mine plus my three grandchildren I had mothered. We had shared so many of the same things in our lives. We had a wonderful day.

Three days before I was to leave, Vic brought up the subject of his apartment. "If we were to marry here, you would have to purchase an apartment also. At that point instead of having the two apartments, we would be able to exchange them for one that would be larger than I have now. I know you can't afford to do this, so I am suggesting I look for another apartment outside of this place."

I suddenly understood since the second day we were together and I had told him about my income, he had known all this and had decided we had no future way back then.

I refused his offer to look for another place to live as he needed the services his building furnished him—its pool, etc. I comforted myself by believing he would find another woman who would fit his life better, and they would have a wonderful end of life together. I could think no other way. I loved the man so much. He sat and shook his head at my refusal.

The following day, I was aware he returned to the building's manager to seek a possible answer for us. On his return, he had nothing to say. I realized Vic had had extra money all his educated life. He lived unaware of the status of many of us. We often manage necessary circumstances beyond our control. This keeps us from gathering piles of dough to clap our hands over. Vic had no idea I would walk into his door, an old woman living on her social security.

Our last days together were not easy as the two of us silently dealt with the fact we were not to be each other's. The wine was still poured, and the evening routine followed. However, we no longer sat side by side on the couch. He drove me up to see the lodge in the mountains but refused to explore it with me. He claimed it would be too hard on his legs. He used a walker constantly.

Another trip was into down town to explore Tacoma's endless bookstore and to meet its owner. Again, Vic remained in the car most of our visit. Our last evening together, he drove across town to take me to dinner at his favorite spot. It was as if we were attending an enormous farewell event despite both of our efforts to be fun and happy. We both did our best to play our part.

The next morning, he followed me with my luggage out of the apartment, down the hall, toward the elevator. I heard him whistle through his teeth as young men will do when they spot a woman of interest walking the street near them. I didn't allow myself to react.

We made it to the lobby and its large entry. Out on the sidewalk, he watched as the waiting cabbie loaded my bag and me into his bright-yellow cab. Vic stood, arms crossed, leaning against the brick wall ten feet away and watched me leave. No kiss was thrown with his wave. Not a word was spoken the whole time.

I realized he was silently endeavoring not to make a heartbreaking scene. Vic had spent his life reaching out to others with understanding help. This time he had failed in something he didn't want to end. Yet he knew he could never make love to me and like a man he felt I shouldn't have to live in such a manner.

I wished as a man he would have let me help him resolve our problem. I deeply cared for him. I was completely heartbroken. My heart was shattered.

Letters were exchanged during the next three weeks. First they were encouraging. He suggested we take time off and allow ourselves to reaccess our feelings. Were they what we thought? He told of visiting his son and daughter-in-law to ask them for their thoughts on a way to bring me back.

Again, I found myself laboring with the heartbreaking loss of money on the sale of our home. With it in my pocket, I would be with Vic. But at my age, one has learned not to deal with such a crazy what-if. The money was gone.

The one positive thought about its loss is Ed. Deep in his Alzheimer's, he never realized the money he had worked many years to earn, saved in investments and real estate, had vanished. He died believing I would be well taken care of as long as I lived.

After I had been home for two weeks, Vic sent me a long letter in which he concluded I should continue my search and to help me he would no longer read any mail he received. It was a firm good-bye.

Its last paragraph made it beyond any response.

> So, my dear, despite the wonderful days we had together, the places we enjoyed, the words we shared and all the things we did in becoming each other's, there are things beyond our reach such as where to live that will not allow us to be together. I love you so much I want you to have a life with a man near you where you can be with your family. The only way this will happen is for you to forget me. To help you do this, I must ask you not to continue reaching out to me. I will not open any letter you send. May your world be wonderful.
>
> Vic

I had thought everything out before climbing into cyberspace. I was ready to move, no matter the distance. I was renting an apartment so had no home to give up as most the men I corresponded did. My family was spread all across the land. Only one lived nearby, and with her five little ones, I saw little of her. Besides, there were trains and airplanes as well as my car. For me, my search had nothing to do with gaining wads of money. I had shared this with every man who got serious with me. Yet it seems to me they didn't listen or understand.

I was devastated after reading his letter. My inability to have the money to enable this wonderful man add me to his remaining years was beyond anger or hurt. Added to this was the damnable distance problem which time after time rears its idiotic head online. Vic was absolutely right when speaking of the wonderful possibilities there would be for us if we were within walking or even driving distance of each other. If there, I could have had a little apartment of my own, and we could have enjoyed each other as frequently as we might have chosen.

It was then I realized that online services can be like casinos—a place we were told would change our world but never informed of the odds.

Even today as I write my story, I can't believe all the old, old men who are living such lonely lives in our great country (their families are not shoving them into care homes) who have lost their sense of discovery and adventure. They are glued to their computers and have a jillion reasons they can't move. Still seven-second maniacs, they have accepted the imaginary for the real.

Where was my gallant hero on his mighty horse?

I cried. I remember it all vividly. It was more than I could handle. I saw no answers. Normally not a cry-baby, especially after all the losses I had experienced in my life, I simply could not stop crying after Vic's loving good-bye.

I decided to move down to Cadillac the next week if Nancy could find me a place to live. I didn't care what it might have to offer in services and extracurricular opportunities. I just wanted a place to hide and wait as my mother did—to die. I decided to write all my men to tell them of my decision and thank them for their friendship. I couldn't write Vic as he had firmly stated we should have no further communication. He couldn't take it. He would not open it.

To this very day, I often think of Vic, wondering what his life has been these last four years. Is he still living? If so, is he alone or with a love? Obviously I did not move to Cadillac to wait to die. Nancy agreed to help me move but discovered the first available housing was five months away. Unknown to me something else was waiting.

24

Coffee Date

It is hard to make myself think about the Anne I was back in early November 2010, a woman who had lost it all. Losing Vic was a deeper loss than any of the others. We had had such an unbelievably wonderful time on all our journeys. Thinking back, I realize Vic had kept his promises he had offered me except the one to marry. The failure of the experiment caused him to believe he wasn't worth my love. Then he had found all those rent excuses.

I had come to believe online dating was only for the young. I was devastated.

Then a phone call from a man who lived in a small town about forty miles southeast of me arrived. I didn't know him other than what I had read online. This had been before Vic. Once Vic began writing me, I completely forgot about Mr. Gaylord.

Before I'd met Vic, I'd been trying to get the e-mails to function between Mr. G. and myself. He had asked if we could telephone instead. His hands were severely arthritic and managing to use a computer's keyboard was all but impossible. There would be far fewer keys to push for him to use his phone.

The two of us had made contact once by phone, but I was so taken with Vic's letters which had started to arrive I simply had let the Gaylord man float off into space.

After a month of silence he was back on my line. His voice had an accent, at least I guessed you could call it so. It was unfamiliar to me. Otherwise, it was low and very pleasant.

"Anne? This is Roy"

"Yes, how are you today?"

"Just fine. I am wondering if we can meet. Have coffee. What about meeting me at Culvers?"

I paused, wondering if I wanted to go. Hadn't I decided I was through with online dates? Hearing no answer, Roy asked me how I was going to know him if I didn't? He then told me people who knew him liked him. He thought I would also.

I heard my inner voice advising me. It pointed out how lonely he sounded, and I had no reason not to go have a cup of coffee and help him brighten his day.

"Anne," he said, "I know you will like me."

"Sounds like a good idea, Roy. I'll see you at the Culver. Name the time."

I thought that Roy would be like the other men I'd met. It is always the same invitation for the woman to meet the men on their turf, rather than the man going to meet the women near their home. How different from the days I dated back in the thirties. My high school senior prom date drove all the way from his home in Cleveland, Ohio. I was living in Sylvania then, more than a hundred miles away. And he had to use his family's car.

It had been a few years since I had been to Gaylord. Before our Mary died of cancer at thirty-nine, leaving her three children with Ed and me, she lived in Michaway Subdivision, south of Gaylord. I had visited her and the grandchildren frequently. Twenty plus years had passed, and I was certain the town had grown.

I double-checked the location of the Culver Inn as it had been built since those times. Roy told me it was across the street from the vets. He would be parked outside the inn in his Escape, which was dark gray. A small stuffed white dog would be on its dashboard. "Not very long after my Mary died, my little Buddy died too. Our Christy gave me the little toy to help me ease my loss." He told me.

"I'll be wearing a red jacket and hat," I told him. As an afterthought, I added, "I am five foot seven, and my hair is gray. I drive a red Focus."

After Roy's call, I actually felt good about having said yes to him. My perspective on the day changed, although I wouldn't realize it until the next morning. I found myself admitting it would be nice to have a local friend to visit and chat with once in a while.

Even though I hadn't fulfilled my dream, I recognized I felt better than when I had started online. I told myself it wasn't going to hurt me to occasionally write some of the men I had enjoyed being with in cyberspace.

I found myself getting excited about climbing in the Focus and having someplace to head. It'd be cold, but no snow was forecast. I would be home long before dark.

As I drove over to meet Roy, I turned south on 131 toward Elmira Hill. Just beyond its top, I would turn left onto Thirty-Two and on into Gaylord by way of the little village of Elmira. The valley between rolling hills would be flat. Acres and acres of potato fields would be planted the next spring tuning the land green.

If I didn't turn onto Thirty-Two just past Deadman's Hill, the Jordan River National Fish Hatchery would be on my right, and the state highway would lead into the hustle and bustle of Michigan's lower region. Just driving this scenic route brought back memories. There was the trip to Clayton's at the foot of the beautiful Appalachians. Three months later, it was Chicago to the national women's meeting and Don for lunch. Next was the almost meet with Dude in Tulsa when I visited my granddaughter and her family for Christmastime. Then Vic's out on the west coast and the life I almost found but was never to be.

Each venture was done with high expectations and determination, yet despite wonderful times and places, nothing was accomplished beyond fun and the opportunity to cement a friendship.

My turn onto M32 to head for Culver's for coffee with Roy brought back the familiar world of potato fields, Elmira's little group of homes, stores, and restaurants. My world was back with me. The beautiful forest, rolling hills, and small lakes covered with winter's first snowfall erased my failures and disappointments. A serenity which only the outdoor world can wrap around one filled me with contentment.

I recognized I was not at all the woman I'd been as I held Ed's hand his last night with me. It wasn't I'd changed into someone else. No, that woman was still down inside of me.

The deepening of my recognition of others and their needs had layered itself onto the older Anne. The new awareness of what makes a man so different from a woman had broadened my ability to reach out and speak to one I didn't even know. Like women, each seemed like the other but was entirely different.

As I sit here and think back to the day I drove over to Gaylord, I believe the most important discovery I had made was that a human never loses the need for love or their ability to love. It was what my brother endeavored to explain to me about men when he quoted to me the seven-second thoughts of them.

I had come to recognize I too harbored the same desire. Yet as a woman, I kept it to myself until I could be with the man of my heart. I had come to understand deep love descends not just onto the young but at anytime in one's lifetime. Yes, even in the eighties and nineties.

My thinking as I drove to meet Roy came to an abrupt halt as I entered Gaylord. Ahead was a mile-long stretch of new commerce in which I was to locate Culvers Inn. After three trips up and down the mile-long jumble of businesses, it became twenty minutes past our meeting time. It was then I finally spotted the inn. Its sign was on the roof not by the street. No one stood by its entrance.

25

My Thank-You

I parked and climbed out of my car only to hear, "Anne?"

Turning, I spotted an old man climbing out of his dark-gray Escape. He waved and slowly headed my way.

"Anne?"

I nodded my head, smiling, I asked, "Roy?"

"I was just about ready to give up and head home."

Looking at his smiling face, I realized he no longer appeared old to me, but rather amazingly handsome for someone in their late eighties. It was his smile, great eyes, and beautiful wavy white hair as well as his active appearing body. No, Roy was not old.

My thoughts were interrupted as he told me, "Culvers had filled up, so we'll go over to Starbucks and enjoy a coffee together."

Locking my car, I climbed in his and road across a lengthy and crowded parking lot to the coffee shop. I admitted to myself Roy didn't appear a fit for me. He was no taller than I was. However, his smile and easy manner were so comfortable, after over an hour of talking back and forth across the tiny coffee table I did not hesitate to accept his invitation to climb back in his car.

"I want to head south of Gaylord ten miles to give you the chance to see my home on Birch Lake," he explained as we headed for his car.

He obviously loved it and wanted to share its beauty with me. His pride of turning a small cottage into a lakeside home oozed out of him. I felt sad when he confided in me he had it listed for sale. When his Mary died, he had seen no other path.

Once sold, his plan was to give his three living children each a quarter of the money. The last quarter would be his. That way, the government would not take some of it in taxes. He was considering moving into the Gaylord retirement home to be with others his age. His loneliness was more than he could handle.

My mind went back to those days when I set out to explore online dating. I was told by many to never, absolutely never accept an invitation to enter an online man's home. Yet there I stood smiling to myself. My experiences had taught me far more about the whole process than most realize they lack. I knew I was absolutely safe. Roy was respecting me as an appreciated guest.

Our hour-long conversation taught me much about the unique man Roy was. His wife, Mary, had succumbed to Alzheimer's as Ed but three months later. They were married sixty-four years, Ed and I sixty-five. Roy was eighty-four, the same age as Vic. And Roy had had more extensive health problems than Vic.

In his fourteenth year of remission, he was taking daily meds for prostate cancer. Yes, like almost all men online who become interested in a gal, the subject of the world of prostrate is discussed if it is present.

He added to this, "My hands and feet were deeply damaged from a bout of arthritis. But unlike the majority who suffer from the decease, it causes no pain. Why I am so fortunate, I have no answer.

"Then I had two bad falls during the past two years. One off a ladder broke a leg and one misstep off a curb caused a broken arm."

Despite all this, Roy never referred to any aches or pains. Like every man I had learned to know online, Roy felt the need to honestly disclose his health issues.

"I feel lucky I can report only having trouble getting up out of a chair or climbing stairs," I answered. I never mentioned my improbable heart attack. After all, there was absolutely nothing wrong with my heart. I just had had a weakened vein that collapsed.

Roy assured me he took his meds and made his visits to the doctor when scheduled.

Just as I had had four children, Roy and his wife, Mary, also produced two sons and two daughters. His namesake and oldest son died at thirty-eight of cancer. Our Tom and Mary had died at forty-two and thirty-nine of cancer. We had that in common.

But it was Roy's love of the wilderness that really drew me in, just as Vic's had. Yet Roy's experiences had been more similar to mine. They involved the Upper Peninsula of Michigan and Canada rather than the far west.

26

Unforeseen Kiss

Ray's home was just that—a snug, homey two-bedroom lakeside cottage. Not an apartment in a large retirement center. It clung to a twenty-foot slope dropping down to the shoreline. Across the waterside, a long porch deck hung over the lawn below. Giant birch and pines clasped their hands overhead as I stood with Roy and gazed across the small lake. Not frozen it's all but black surface laid like a mirror in the early afternoon sun. A family of ducks slowly swam by about twenty feet off shore.

Close by birdfeeders were being visited by wrenches, finches, and nuthatches. I found myself entranced and reluctant to admit the cold air was beginning to suggest I take Roy's invitation to go back into the house and warm up.

Inside, he showed me how he had added to the original small cottage to produce the lovely home he and his Mary retired to from way down state some twenty-five years before. A huge antlered deer head brought forth stories of younger years when hunting and fishing were his passions. "This one," he said pointing to it hanging on the living room wall, "I shot with a bow and arrow in the Upper Peninsula."

At that, the two of us were off telling stories of our camping and fishing ventures, one memory leading to another. It was late afternoon before we realized how time had flown. Roy asked, "What if I take you out for dinner at a restaurant near your parked car before you head home? I'm concerned about your arriving there safely before night fall."

This is typical thinking about us older women. We aren't to be out in the dark.

We were on our way quickly and shared a great meal at a Chinese restaurant. Then he headed me back to my car. As I prepared to climb out of his, without a thought, I turned to thank him for a wonderful afternoon and planted a small peck on the corner of his mouth. In surprise, Roy jerked back, causing his cap to fall on the floor.

I couldn't believe what I'd done. Never in all my long life had I ever pulled such a thing.

"Oh, Roy, I'm sorry." As he searched for his cap, I quickly left his car and hurried into mine. I shook my head at myself all the way home and long after. I couldn't find a why for what I'd done. I realized a peck on a cheek is a natural thank-you by friends all over the world and holds no other meaning. My concern was how Roy perceived it.

Two weeks passed with only a couple of e-mail tries by Roy and they didn't arrive intact. I was over my head with the mental turmoil of whether to ask Nancy to continue to look for a retirement center down near her to help remove Vic from my mind. Or should I simply move from my two bedrooms into a cheaper one-bedroom in my complex. Just thinking about it brought tears to my eyes.

I e-mailed Roy to tell him I wouldn't be available for coffee again as I was moving to another apartment before Christmas. The phone rang, and to my surprise, it was Roy.

"Anne, I am wondering if you'd like to come over here for dinner with me tonight. I plan to have chicken, and I am a good cook. I promise you will like it."

Before I could answer, he added, "The weather is supposed to stay good—no snow for a while."

I couldn't have been more surprised. Yet the idea of getting out of the apartment and all its mess to have someone share a meal with sounded perfect. I heard myself saying yes and asking about the time. After hanging up, I decided to bake an apple pie to take along—it had been a long time since I'd had a reason to do so.

Roy proved to be an excellent cook, and my pie made a big hit. His favorite music, country Western, softly filled the rooms. We talked without stopping, further discovering each other. His had been the life of a big city boy who was born of a Canadian mother who came to this country to marry. His father died when he was five. A grandmother plus many uncles and aunts joined forces to give him places to call home and grow into a teenager.

He recalled how at ten his mother, covered in a blood-spattered nightgown, woke him to leave their house. His stepfather had severely beaten her. When he reached the eighth grade, he was misdiagnosed with TB and withdrawn from school, never to be returned.

His effort to enlist in the service in WWII was denied due to the lung scar which had been misdiagnosed. He was thrown into the world of minimum wage employment shoveling coal at eighty cents an hour. No family member suggested completing his education. But back in those days, attending school beyond the eighth grade was not considered necessary by many. Over the years, Roy self-educated himself with an intense love of reading and keen understanding of those he worked for.

But there were similarities. Both Roy and I married young. Our marriages had been long and full of love. Our children were our pride. Although not a church attendee, Roy was a believer as I was. The outdoor world and all it contained was special to both of us. Those we knew and didn't were important. Money was necessary, yet not our goal. Our age was an unbelievable gift to us both.

Our long conversations had begun upon my arrival and didn't end until Roy suddenly said, "Anne, I had no idea it was so late. Look out the window. The sun is going down."

I turned me head toward the large window staring out across the deck, the lake and to the hills beyond. There was the golden sun sinking behind them.

His arm encircled my waist as we stood looking out over all of nature. He turned to me and said, "There is no way you are driving home in the dark. Not on these winter roads. I hope you will stay here and make the trip back to Boyne in the morning."

Turning to the hallway, he said, "Come with me."

Roy took me into the smaller bedroom and showed me its single bed. Opening a dresser drawer, he pulled out a pair of his PJs. Turning, he handed them to me, saying, "Here, you can wear these tonight. I'll get out a towel, et cetera, for you in the bathroom. I even have an extra toothbrush just in case it might be needed. I'll get breakfast in the morning." There was nothing Roy did or said to indicate he, like most men, couldn't wait to crawl in bed with me.

I slept long and deeply. Breakfast was great.

Winter arrived and with it, Christmas. Roy and I both spent the holiday with our families. Yet a wonderful box of chocolates arrived from Roy. It hadn't entered my head to purchase a gift for him. Never in all my life had I received such a gift before. I was impressed. Not even my Ed had given me candy.

I moved to the one-bedroom apartment. It was less expensive than the one I had before with Ed. In our part of Michigan, above the forty-fifth parallel, the days have long dark evenings during which no television show, musical rendition, or book dissolves the loneliness of being alone. Roy's smile, conversation, home in Michigan's wilderness, his wit, and love brought my wholeness back to me.

At first I tried to schedule my visits two days with Roy and the rest of the week in Boyne. However, I'd be home a day and Roy would call to ask when I would be returning that evening. He'd have dinner ready.

With no reason to stay put, I would pack and head southeast. It seemed so wonderful to be in a home rather than a dark apartment. There I contently repaired a beautiful old handmade quilt Roy's niece had made him. It was the old "trip around the world" design composed of countless two-inch squares of flowery calico. He used it as his bed cover. It brought back to me the days my Mary had helped me sell my quilt patterns I designed across the country and in England. We had had such great times.

I baked great pumpkin and apple pies and made various hearty soups—neither were something I'd ever make when living alone. His laptop filled my computer needs, and the little church at the nearby Michawey subdivision welcomed me on Sunday mornings. My daughter Nancy had served as its pastor one year and our Mary had attended it before she died.

I painted his portrait and the lake beyond the dining room window. He prepared breakfast and my morning tea. We took off for the grocery, doctor appointments, and occasional dinner out. His brother, a nearby neighbor, stopped by almost daily at 10:00 a.m. to visit. We read or talked of memories. I met those who lived nearby. We fell in love.

27

No Music

Our first meet had been on November 11, 2020. It was after Christmas Roy pulled a surprise on Valentine day by driving us into Gaylord and with my help selected an engagement ring. Yes, I left the store engaged to my Roy. He assigned me his pretty second bedroom and our life began together. To top this off he received the huge surprise of a request to purchase his home within the same week. By the end of May with his brother's and my Paul and Nancy's help we found ourselves moved into a beautiful two bedroom home on South Lake Street in Boyne City. It was perfect for Roy as it stood beneath tall maple trees and looked to the west across huge Lake Charlevoix. Our sunsets were fabulous as his had been back below Gaylord over his little lake. We so enjoyed being together out on our backyard deck.

Yes, we gathered what was ours. His large hutch sat in the living room as his desk and mine stood in the dining room as my family antique display. We purchased a new comfy couch to use in front of our big fireplace and TV. There we could cuddle and enjoy music, favorite shows and each other. We were settled in time to offer our home to Rachael and Rutt for a gathering place following their wedding out on Lake Charlevoix's shore in Horton Bay on June 11th. It wasn't much later Roy established a backyard garden for me and parked our motor home beside it. Yes, he had fulfilled a long time dream. We journeyed all summer long. He then chose November 11, the end of our first year together to be our wedding day. My Pastor Paul and Nancy performed a Church Blessing ceremony for us in h is beautiful old Presbyterian Church in Cadillac. What a day to remember!

We both lost all our years—we became young and deeply in love. Although Roy had his prostate problem, it never interfered with our passionate lovemaking. He became one of Clayton's great "tuners."

Roy was fascinated in learning the process. After my one time with Vic, I was a darn good teacher. As we discussed our lifetime loves, I had discovered Roy's Sally had moved him out of their bedroom into the guest room shortly after their last daughter was born. She wanted no more of his loving. She turned to reading late in the evenings before crawling in her bed alone. I suspected she found her "love" in the large number of romantic novels available for women in those days. I was thrilled I could bring back the world of lovemaking to my Roy.

Different as night and day, we both immediately realized we had done various every day type of things radically differently. Neither of us cared if we leaned one way or the other in how it was to be done for us. Never in all my long years of married life had my breakfast been prepared for me. I was always in the kitchen getting things ready when our family arrived downstairs.

With Roy, I was in bed happily asleep until he entered to wake me up at nine with a kiss, "Time to join me, darling. Your tea is waiting." Then he'd crawl in with me, and it was usually about ten when we made it to my tea.

Roy also brought music into my life. It was to be heard as I joined him at the table for breakfast and on through the day. Not invasive, just background. I found myself humming, dancing on my feet as I stood doing things or keeping time with my fingers as I sat or read.

It was always country songs, and I discovered how American they really were. Some were so deeply thoughtful and encouraging, others silly, or heartbreaking and almost tearful. They reminded me of life's ups and downs. Others brought Roy to me, arms outreaching, "My darling woman, come dance with me." Wrapped within his arms, we would dance, whether in the kitchen, dining, or living room.

Oh, we had our favorites. On the top of them all was Ray Price's "For the Good Times." Back in our early days together when we were just discovering our love, Roy would call me at my apartment to ask me to come over. He would say, "Please come over, Anne. I have dinner ready for you.'

But, when I picked up the phone before I heard Roy's voice, the words of "For the Good Times" would flow into my ear. And there was the sad one of Bobby Bare's "Streets of Baltimore." Add Jim Reeves's "One Thousand Three Hundred Yards to Go" and Bob Dylan's "Five Hundred Miles." For the two of us who so loved the outdoors and wilderness, the music was perfect. There were times when I did floor dance shows for Roy, he so loved to laugh with me as I flipped about.

Our kitchen was small and narrow. All the cupboards, sink, and stove were along the outside window wall. Oh, the view of our little eight-foot square vegetable garden Roy had made for me out of railroad ties was fun to watch as it grew. All around its outer edge (forty-eight feet) was a single row of sweet onions. Roy had arrived home from the hardware with a big bag of them he had bought—hundreds. They framed the corn, potatoes, tomatoes, cabbage, herbs, etc. It was my love. Roy kept it watered, and I weeded it.

The wall opposite way our laundry, the refrigerator filled one end opposite the door into the dining room. Next to it was the pantry door. Inside, I stored all the food and gadgets we shared. Roy added great storage shelving on the inside of its door. There my spices and his cereal were easy to grab.

But his greatest idea was to use the dishwasher tucked in next to the sink not for doing the dishes but to use to store all the pans, kettles, and skillets we were constantly using. Bending over to find them hidden in the lower cupboards was just too difficult for both of us. Hand washing our few dishes was no job.

We compared our time together as that of a couple of teenagers, not the antiques we truly were. Unlike our earlier married days, he did not have to leave for work each morning nor did I have to raise children and worry about their future. They were away in their own lives, and Roy had done his bit in the work world. Every hour of every day and night were ours to share and enjoy. Admittedly, we had not perceived this radical difference in our lives and found it unbelievable. It was difficult to understand.

All those years, Ed and I had invaded the wilderness Roy had fished and hunted. After his retirement, he longed to purchase a motor vehicle and camp, but his Mary said no.

When he discovered my love of the outdoors, he proceeded to explore the world of motor homes. After four different sizes and shapes, he found our "Ben" and off we went. All over the Upper Peninsula, we explored one state park after another as well as hanging out in Mel's and her Jim's side yard way up north. It was heaven.

Our favorite park was a small state forest campground, Little Hog Island, on the northern shore of Lake Michigan about sixty miles west of the Mackinac Bridge. It had been my destination with Ed and our children many times. I have many paintings of it with its tiny island not far off shore. Just recently, I gave my son-in-law one of them to use for the cover of his new book of grief poems he wrote and published following our Nancy's death two years ago. She was sixty.

Because of all the memories Roy and I had about roaming about the Upper Peninsula in our motor home, I suggested to him we celebrate our first wedding anniversary on November 11 in our motor home where it was parked for the winter beyond the veggie garden in our backyard. Roy got excited about the idea and sent me off to the edge of town to pick up hamburgers and such while he warmed up "Ben" (I had named it), got the table ready, and the radio filling its interior with our favorite music.

I went off for the goodies and brought them back to Ben. We dove in laughing at ourselves—so excited about our anniversary celebration in the motor home on a November day. Just as we were finishing our sandwiches and starting on the ice cream, a loud crash fell down on us from above. Buckets of water slammed the windows, walls, and roof. Then it was thunder—all unbelievable! We were trapped. There was no way we could penetrate the unexpected storm and make it to the house. We were trapped!

After three hours on the couch-bed, we were able to get into the house. What a celebration—unforgettable—as the year ahead of us would become.

Despite his prostate problems, Roy had himself a great time, and of course, I did also. But spending the night in bed together was impossible as he claimed I snored. Eventually this changed. I don't think it had anything to do with my snoring. No, it just reached the point we longed to be in each other's arms as we slept. Our love deepened as the days rolled by much to our disbelief.

It took us back all those years to our early days of marriage and the time we were with our original spouses. We talked of them and things we had done. Roy told me of the times his eyes roamed and he cheated on his Mary. I told him I never suspected my husband had a wandering eye, but then such things weren't talked about, so why would I have?

Ed's and my love had been every other night all through the first fifty years of our long marriage. It was when Ed had surgery in his lower area for what I thought was an urination problem his lovemaking suddenly stopped.

All I could blame it on was his age and his having to stop at all Michigan's roadside parks to relieve himself. No one talked about prostate in those days. Our last eighteen years of marriage had been without intimacy, but our love never weakened.

In fact, it was the deep love we shared to the very end that inspired me to go online. I wanted to have it back, never dreaming it would return as intensely as Roy brought it. When I remembered Clayton, Will, and Vic, I felt sorry for them because they had not accepted the fact that love between a man and woman in their eighties and nineties really could be deep and rich.

Roy and I occasionally talked about our ages and the fact one of us would eventually reach their termination. We would nod our heads in agreement and drop the subject, knowing it was completely beyond our control.

Looking each other in the eye, we would say, "I understand it's around the corner, but that makes our being together today even more wonderful. We will be side by side when the time comes for good-byes, not alone in some rest home."

And so it came about. Despite his younger age, Roy was the one to leave shortly before his eighty-ninth birthday and our third anniversary on November 11, 2014. This seemed unfair to me as I was two years the senior.

One morning in early December 2013, he came back into our bedroom to wake me up and tell me. "Honey, I can't eat anything. Something is wrong. Will you drive me to the hospital?"

Off we went. After extensive tests performed in emergency, I was told he had cancer of the lower esophagus. If I hadn't brought him in, he would not have been with me in ten or eleven days.

The situation was so severe surgery was performed the following day, on a Saturday. A feeding tube was inserted below the lower esophagus. With it, I would feed him liquids only as he progressed through chemotherapy and radiation treatments.

That year, northern Michigan suffered the most severe winter and snowfall for over fifty years. Through it all, I drove him up and down the eighteen miles of hills to and from the hospital almost daily. Despite our fervent prayers, not enough remedy was accomplished through all the treatments. In early March, Roy was sent home under the care of hospice and me to go through his final days.

We were told cancer existed in his lungs also, and because of his age and the lack of success with the esophagus, they could not extend his treatments. Unbelievably, he had no pain. Many years before he had quit smoking. Once he decided to, it had taken him one day.

His love for food never left him. He spoke so longingly for his favorite dinners, urging me, "Please fix yourself a chicken dinner tonight with all your wonderful side dishes, especially gravy and broccoli." This was so he could relish their smell. Early on, he might accept a teensy bit, but soon not so. It broke my heart.

Eventually, he no longer had any desire to sit on our back deck to watch the lake or the birds. Nor did he snuggle on the couch with me to watch our favorite TV shows—*Wheel of Fortune* and *Jeopardy* or any sports.

Then, unbelievably, he asked, "Honey, please turn off the music." I couldn't believe his request. Slowly, the days passed by us silently. Weeks and months went with them.

After eight months, he was receiving oxygen through a breathing tube, sitting in a recliner and used a wheelchair to move down the hall to the bathroom. Despite it all, we climbed into bed together, air tube and all. Our love was sustaining both of us. His illness was affecting him not only physically but emotionally. Everything he loved so deeply such as music he had dropped, but not me.

Father's Day in June surprised us with the totally unexpected arrival of his two daughters, one of their husbands, and Roy's son, Frank. How wonderful of them to make the drives. Thanks to our beloved motor home in the backyard, we had room for them all.

The fall before seated in our motor home, I had asked, "What if next summer we head out to Yellowstone National Park in Ben? We could head north into the Upper Peninsula."

Roy immediately agreed. "We'll follow its southern highway route 2 along the north shore of Lake Michigan westward. Driving slowly we'll use as much of the summer as needed."

It was hard to accept our inability to fulfill our dream. Roy repeatedly told me, "I wish I could have had one more good year with you." I echoed his wish. There would be tears in both our eyes.

Much to my complete surprise as the weekend drew to a close, we understood the oldest daughter's husband, she was about sixty-eight, and her brother were leaving for home and their work. One of them took the motor home with him. Roy had given it to him.

The two daughters were staying on with their father. Trish was fifteen years younger than her sister, Mel. The strange thing to me was neither had come to their father or me to determine if their plan was something we would appreciate. They apparently felt I would be all for it. And I was. Their love for their father was so special. The girls would be on hand to help me. I was thrilled with their decision. Knowing how dearly Roy loved his daughters, I believed their love would help him through his days yet ahead.

28

Without a Question

About three weeks before they appeared on the scene, I had discussed with Roy what he thought I should do once he left. Our landlord had called to say he could continue renting to us as long as Roy was still in need of a home. But once Roy died, he was being forced to place the house on the market to cover some debt he owed. We understood and thanked him.

There was absolutely no way we could afford to buy the house, much as we loved it. For just one, it would have been way too large and expensive. The rent plus all its utilities would be out of reach of my monthly Social Security check. I would have to seek a small apartment in town.

That had been something I had done as my Ed's death approached. Because of this, I knew where to go and how to place my name on lists to wait for a vacancy. As I had done previously, I rented a small storage garage on the south edge of town in which to stash the boxes I would pack in preparation for my move.

I would do it out of Roy's sight in my bedroom so not to depress him any further. He would assume I was writing as my computer was in there. I couldn't think of anything harder to involve myself in. Yet I realized it was necessary as Roy was slowly leaving me.

How I would have loved his daughters' help! But none was offered, even though they knew what I was up to. They spent their time watching TV, doing crossword puzzles, and other games, or their laptop.

Roy suggested I move myself into the new retirement center in Boyne City following his departure. "Now, dear, you know I am not ready for that. I want to be able to have my car to drive places I like to go. For instance when I want to go paint, it is out into the country," I reminded him.

Slowly our garage began to fill with tubs. In turn, I lifted them into my little Ford and lugged them out to the storage garage. Some were definitely on the heavy side, and I scolded myself for struggling with them. The girls ignored my work.

Suddenly, one day, Mel began to feed Roy his five times a day "meals." When I asked her to please let me feed Roy, she informed me she had worked in such a position in a care center for twenty-eight years and knew just what to do. I tried to explain to her I also knew, I had been at it for seven months, and Roy was doing far better than hospice had ever dreamed he would. The hospice nurses couldn't believe he'd lasted as long as he had and they believed part was because of the good care I'd given him.

Plus, when I fed him, it was an opportunity for the two of us to be together. I treasured the time. Roy slept most of his remaining hours. The daughter would not budge.

I was at a complete loss as to what I could do to put the two women at ease and be part of our family. I had just lost my remaining daughter, Nancy at sixty, the spring before because of an extremely rare heart condition. Medical science had not succeeded in treating the problem. I would have loved to have Roy's girls as mine.

The best I could do was let Mel and Trish have their way, and I did so by keeping busy with my writing, packing, and time with Roy. I could squeeze it in whenever he was awake. This became more and more difficult as one or the other of the girls would take over my chair beside him. This left me the one across the room from him. There could be none of our treasured hand holding then.

They slowly took over the telephone answering and hospice when it arrived to see Roy. I felt like someone from somewhere else, almost a visitor.

Roy spoke to me about their behavior. He pleaded, "Anne, my darling, don't fight with them."

I knew he was right. His emotions as well as his health were dissolving more each day. I realized Roy more than any of us needed smiles and peace in the air about him.

Holding his hand, I replied, "Darling man, you know I don't believe in fighting. I love your daughters. They are the only ones I have. I am so lucky."

Much to my surprise, about then, I began to get notices from one of the online services I had used three years earlier. A "poke" had arrived for me. This made no sense as I had cancelled my memberships back in January 2011.

Clicking on, I discovered the very same profile as I had used during my earlier online researching. The only difference was my age. It was ninety-one instead of eighty-six as it had been back in 2009. How could the computer service know I was still living?

I tried to find a way to contact the service but had no success. Every day, I continued to receive notice of pokes. Then the thought came to me I would write each knock on my door by explaining I was an online researcher. I would keep their name to notify them when I had all the answers I was searching for. My list became longer and longer. They all backed off.

One eventually arrived from an eighty-eight-year-old Boyne City man who complimented me on my looks and how much he enjoyed reading my newspaper column. He had heard of my present life situation, and if I needed help to please let him know. I replied, thanking him for his offer but said I was doing okay. He responded a couple more times, and I simply said, "No, but thanks."

July was nearing its last days when Mel and Trish came in the living room one morning with their hands clenched and on their hips. Their shoulders were thrown back; dark anger lined their face.

I was seated beside Roy. We were holding hands and traveling through memories of things we had done together. Of fun, surprises, adventures, and people who had woven themselves into our time with each other.

As I turned to look up at his daughters, fear flew into me. I couldn't believe the hatred lining their faces as they chorused to me, "Get away from our father. He is our father, our mother's husband, not yours. We want you out of here. Out right now! You horrible, black, nasty old woman! You are nothing but a dark, evil woman who has tried to steal our father from all that is his! Get out! Get Out! He is through with you, you evil, dark contriving woman! Go! Go!"

"We know you are online looking for another man to steal from his family. Well, you aren't doing this to our dad. Get out of here!"

I tried to stay calm. "You are wrong," I told them. "I am not online. Somehow it has been sending me notices, but I only reply to secure the name and address of each to notify them when my online research is complete. I am making a marketing list. I have no idea how this online business started up for me again."

I tuned to look at Roy and his face was that of a very sick man who had just been struck down. His eyes looked at me in deep despair.

He murmured, "They asked me for your password. I gave it to them. After all, they are my beloved daughters. I trusted them."

"Do you want me to leave?" I asked him.

His head moved and his chin almost touched his chest, but his squinting eyes told me his answer was yes.

I leaned over and whispered in his ear. "I will be with you every minute in love."

His eyes gleamed his love back to me.

Turning back to the daughters, I told them. "I will be out by morning."

Their response was instant. "Then Dad will sleep in his recliner here in the living room with us tonight. You aren't going to be in bed with him ever again."

Not together a last time? No time to tell him my love would be with him wherever he might be? Or of all his family who will be waiting for him up in the world above us. No one can describe this to us, yet it is our promise. I pictured my Nancy with her arms outstretched to welcome him. The week before she had died the preceding June she had asked him to take good care of me after she left this world. None of us ever foresaw his daughters' hatred.

At this point, Mel stepped forward to thrust her clenched fist in my face. I quickly swung my head sideways so her hand barely glazed my ear. Miraculously, I was okay.

The two daughters were not allowing their father and me an opportunity to hold each other or even say good-bye. There was to be no parting gesture I hoped would fill his remaining days as well as mine.

They were beyond belief as they stood before me growling and glaring. They saw in me only the woman they had just described despite the wonderful visits we had shared together during the past two summers and the paintings I had done for each of them. No wonder they spoke horribly of their husbands as they did. They simply did not understand men or their love. They wanted their father's money, not him. Yet it was already there for them, not to be mine. He and I had agreed on this.

I realized immediately we had made our mistake by not including our families in how our money would all be theirs once we left the earth.

I turned away saying, "I will be gone before that."

29

Tears

It wasn't Roy's impending death that affected me mentally. No, it was his emotional state of having to have to make his way to his death without me at his side. Yes, his daughters would probably be there unless they moved him into a care center. There was one across the street from the eldest's home. It was where she stuck him for a few months after his Mary's death. After a while, he had chosen to return to his home on the lake. He wasn't ready to leave life. This time he had believed I would be at his side all the way. He had told me if we hadn't married, he was certain he would be in the home by now.

But I wouldn't be at his side with our hands holding each other and our love all about. Roy understood the difference between the love his daughters could give him and the love I would have for him. This whole idea was just too much for me to handle. His death wouldn't be the gentle one we were anticipating.

I had learned back in the years I lost Pat, our Mary's husband, Tom, and then Mary. My sadness knowing they had moved out of my life could not overcome the joy I felt knowing they each had moved on into heaven. I felt the same about Roy and his long illness. I wanted it to end gently for him. I had no tears. How could I feel anything but happiness knowing all my children's suffering was gone and instead they were with those of the family who had already made the journey into the unknown world of heaven? Only if I questioned my belief in heaven could I feel sad.

The fact that heaven is not tangible often leads a person into disbelief. If they can't see it or talk to someone who has been there, it remains impossible for them to accept such a fantastic end to their life. I remember so well way back when I was eighteen and just out of high school. I was working in Mother's rose garden one day with Dad. We were extending her little fence along its edge so she could plant a couple more roses. Out of the blue, he asked, "Anne, do you believe in heaven?"

His question absolutely floored me. My mind simply refused to work out an answer. I stood there in silence. Looking at me, he understood and said, "Oh, honey, you don't need to give me your answer right this moment. We'll talk about it some other time." As I said, I have never forgotten the question and who asked it. Dad never brought the subject up again. Yet all my life I asked myself, "Anne, do you believe in heaven?" Eventually I found my answer but in a manner I would have never dreamed of.

It fell on me in a completely unexpected manner about three months after I had driven back down to Toledo, Ohio, in 1982 to celebrate Mother's eighty-fourth birthday with her. That was the visit during which she told me that her life had not improved during her four years following my Dad's death. Rather she prayed ever morning to die to be with him in heaven. Yes, Mother believed completely in heaven. Yet I never thought to ask her to explain it all to me. Back then I thought my life was all but over. I was sixty years old. That was old in those days.

I was in the wonderful kitchen Ed had built across the back of the old farm house which stood on the beautiful cherry orchard he bought for us to call home. It was just out on the northeast side of Boyne City in Michigan. I was ironing. Standing by my long ironing board in the kitchen's breakfast table bay window, I could see the outdoor world of woods, hillside, and orchards. I loved our home. The telephone rang.

It was my brother's wife, Gloria. She was in the Toledo Hospital with Mother who had gone in the previous week when

Doc discovered her sick in bed in her apartment. Yes, she had had the flu and with no one at her side, badly needed some hospital care. My plan was to drive down the very next day to be with her for a week as she was being released then. I was so excited about being with her when she needed me.

Gloria's voice was full of urgency as she said, "Anne, your mother just died, and I can't find Doc. What should I do?"

I felt like something had hit me. How could Mother be dead? Wasn't I going to be there with her the very next day?

I answered, "Gloria, please calm down. You don't have anything to do. Just be glad you are there with her. The hospital knows exactly what needs to be done. They will locate Doc and he will be with you right away. Find yourself a room where you can sit. Get a cup of coffee to have while you wait. Ed and I will leave here in an hour and be with you this evening."

"But what dress should I get out to put on her?" Gloria asked.

How like her, I thought as I responded, "Let's check out her closet at her apartment to decide that, Gloria. Right now please just sit down and wait for Doc. I am saying good-bye now as I must call Ed so we can get on our way. Our thoughts will be with you. Bye."

I called Ed the immediately and he agreed. He'd get home and we would be on our way, if I'd pack what he would need. As I hung up the telephone, I felt the love I had for my Ed. Our love sustained me no matter what—even this surprise, my Mother's sudden and unexpected death. I hung my phone up and turned to head for the bedroom to pack our suitcase.

As I turned, I saw him. Yes, there stood my father over in the shadows of the stairway. He stood completely dressed in white. It was loose and flowing. And his arms were outreaching toward me. Yet his face, with its enormous smile and excitement, told me it was who was standing behind me, not me they were for. Yes, he was welcoming my mother! He looked so young.

I heard myself calling out to him, "Yes, Dad, now I do believe in heaven."

It is hard for me to believe I said such a thing. But I did. At that instant, I knew heaven existed and my father was there as my mother had believed, waiting for her. I felt her joy and never felt tears in my eyes.

I was sixty years old then. My life had been full of the unexpected time after time. Yet this one moment prepared me for all that lay in my future of which I had no expectations. Yes, the deaths of my children and even Ed and Roy have never filled me with sadness. Understanding where their journey had led them filled me with joy knowing that each one was where we all are told we can be at the end of our life here on earth. I simply could not shed a tear. The pain of their illnesses was gone. The arms of those of their families who had preceded them were wrapped around them. How could I feel anything but joy for them? I know I will be with all of them as my journey here on earth draws to its close. Yes, I pray I will be with them all. And, Dad, I believe I will be. I don't have any idea how it will all happen, but I know it will. Yes, you and I will have our laughs over your question back in Mother's rose garden.

30

Love and Live

Thinking back to the moment I promised the two girls I would leave and never return, it still remains impossible for me to understand just what my mind was doing. I had said good-bye to my beloved hubby at a time he needed me with him more than ever before.

I'm not talking about his physical requirements. Mel had that well in hand. It was the emotional state about his approaching death. The need we had for each other during this anticipated but not acceptable happening in our happy lives was not understood by either of his daughters. Neither Roy nor I wished to bring it about any sooner than his body would do naturally, but with this trauma, we both realized this would be impossible.

I turned my back on it all and walked down our narrow hallway to its first door, my bedroom and office. It was where I secluded the huge research mess I had generated. A computer, files, and all the necessary gear lined one wall of the room. My telephone stood at its far end.

I reached out for it. I would call Pat, my grandson, with his recent law degree and ask his advice. I was certain I knew what his words of wisdom would be, yet I wanted to hear them. I needed to be certain I was making the right decision. Fortunately he was at his desk.

In a panic, I told him what had just happened to Roy and me. I became aware of his disbelief by the change in his voice. "Oh, Grandma, I am so sorry for the two of you. I wish so I was there with you. But knowing you, I won't worry. Those two have met their match."

Although Roy and my wedding had been a church blessing, not a big family affair, we were aware of the deep respect and love my family had for him. I had felt the same about his family.

I breathed a big sigh of relief as Pat confirmed my thinking. Because of Paul and Nancy's church blessing wedding they had set up for us, neither Roy nor I had any legal power. To take the two women to court so I could remain with him would only extend the ugly fighting for months with nothing to gain.

I thanked Pat with all my heart. I strongly suspected Mel and Trish had sought the same knowledge from an attorney. They weren't dummies. Thinking back, I recalled their recent return from a three-day jaunt back to their homes. Mel had arrived with a paper to be notarized. I even had been the one to locate a couple neighbors to walk over and stand through the procedure. I had not been invited to take part.

I shake my head at myself. "How in the world didn't I suspect something was going on behind my back? How could two such nice women harbor such hatred for me?" It didn't bother me. Nothing could. Roy's illness had me completely within its grasp.

No, all this had been carefully thought out and executed. Putting me back online proved that. That had to have been the younger daughter. She lived on her laptop. Mel wouldn't be bothered with one.

As I turned to hang up the phone, I thanked Pat, "I so thank you for your understanding and help, Pat. Thank heaven I have you standing beside me."

I promised to keep Pat posted as I moved forward. I hung up the phone and turned to face my room and all that was mine. It would have to be boxed and transferred to my apartment.

Six weeks earlier while Roy and I were going through the feeding routine hospice had set up, we had lots of time to talk. Most of it was of memories. These produced smiles and even laughter. The things we had done together. Yet at the same time, we let ourselves look down the road to his leaving.

As I had shared with you, his first advice was for me to move into the new senior housing development out by the park. I even went out and picked up their literature. And much to my surprise, I could afford to move there thanks to my ability as a veteran's wife to secure financial assistance. But even so, I would not be able to keep my car because of the cost of its insurance.

Thus it was I had an apartment waiting for all the stuff I was looking at in my bedroom. The Silver Street apartments were the last ones I asked to have my name put on their waiting vacancy list. Instead, the owner said, "I'll have one ready for you, Anne, in two days." I all but fell off my chair in surprise. All the others had advised me it might be six months or longer before one was available.

Included in my office-bedroom was a nine-foot-long and six-foot-high bookshelf loaded with books and memorabilia. I groaned. There was no way I could leave our home by evening and accomplish all I must.

Once again, I picked up the telephone to call a wonderful friend of mine. He was about my remaining son's age, seventy, and leader of the deacons in our church. Through Don, I would seek help in moving.

I realized they couldn't show up within an hour but hopefully within a week. I would leave that day with the understanding with Roy's daughters my things would remain until whatever day the deacons selected to do the work.

Don had become a good friend of Roy's. When he listened to my explanation for the move, he couldn't believe what had happened. His concern was immediately for Roy. "How is Roy taking this, Anne?"

My reply, "Silently, he is devastated. He loves his daughters yet like both of us, Don, can't believe what they are doing."

I removed all the family photos from my bedroom walls and carefully packed them. Next I called my friends, Susie and Pat, asking if I could hang out at their home overnight. I explained why and they were enraged. Their immediate reaction was, "We'll call the police and have the daughters moved out of your house."

"Oh, that's not an option. Remember our marriage was just a church ceremony, not a legal wedding. Doing so isn't an option." They understood.

The following day, Don brought a bed out to the apartment. "This is for you, Anne. It's a keeper. A woman of the church wants you to have it if you have the need."

So I had a bed to sleep in. One's church family is so special. Three days later, a Saturday, ten men and two women arrived to remove all my possessions out of the house and its garage. Even Beth, our minister, was right there in the middle of it all.

A week or so before all this happened, Beth had come to see Roy. He had asked her to sing "Amazing Grace" for him. She was a fantastic vocalist. Much to Roy's delight, she had sung the entire song, absolutely beautiful.

I was overwhelmed with the deacon's help. I had no family within one hundred miles of me except for granddaughter Melissa with five small children. Obviously she couldn't be of much help with those five helping her—the oldest was only eight. Although on the disastrous weekend right before Christmas when I rushed Roy to the hospital and he was diagnosed with cancer, she had abounded her little sweethearts to spend the next three days at Roy's beside. She had almost obtained her nursing degree at that time. There is no way she could understand what a gift she gave me.

The deacons were lifesavers when I thought I might drown. I had a church family beyond belief!

During this entire procedure, both Roy's daughters stood on the sidelines observing it all. Not once did they offer to do a thing. It was as if we were under the surveillance of the police.

We were not going to be allowed to take anything either felt was their father's.

This included those he had purchased for the two of us to enjoy such as his beloved Bose radio. My Pat had bought it for him in the shop where he was working down in Detroit. It disappeared out our deck door and into one of their cars. Our vacuum disappeared. It had been Roy's, but as it was easier to use than my big vacuum, we had given mine away. They didn't know that so it didn't count.

I stayed in the garage and driveway, not emotionally able to go into the house on moving day. I was certain Mel would single me out for a fight if I did. Roy couldn't have that happening. It had been my promise to him not to. It was easy for me to list what it was in the home should go with me. I made one bad error. Two of my favorite paintings I had hung in Roy's bedroom for him to enjoy were forgotten. As a result, I no longer have either.

The following weekend, three of my grandchildren arrived from their distant homes to help me unpack and put away box after box. I became the reciprocator of more love than imaginable. It descended as a comfort on me I needed more than the actual labor.

Every box was opened, and its contents placed in an appropriate spot in my small one-bedroom abode. Laura, the oldest, arranged all my books on the extensive book cases I took with me and stood against one of the living room's long walls. There, for the first time in their long lives, they were arranged as if in a library.

Rachael and Rutt filled cupboards, drawers, and the walls with clothing, dishes, pictures, food, sewing, painting, and office gadgets. Everything they discovered in the boxes had once been part of the home in which Rachael had grown up with Ed and me.

What did I do? Nothing except answer the questions they tossed my way. "Where do you want this put, Grandma?" "Is this going to be okay here in this corner?"

I was overwhelmed with the support I had showered upon me. It quieted my anger and tears. Instead I spoke thanks for it all.

As I'd promised Roy I would do, every night as I crawled into bed, I placed kisses on the two wonderful photos of him on my bed stand. Then I turned and blew one up to his large portrait I had painted back in those early days before he sold his home and moved into Boyne with me.

Once in bed and the covers pulled over myself, I reached out to wrap my arms about him and feel his hands finding me. Only then could I fall asleep. For the first time in my long life I found it difficult to sleep soundly. I woke up almost hourly. Despite this, I was able to return to sleep without having to leave my bed and prowl the apartment.

Roy and I said those brief good-byes July 24. Not once was I allowed to speak with him on the phone or stop by for a brief word. I did get reports from Don and our next door neighbor, Doug, about Roy's progress as a result of their visits with him which the women allowed.

Checking with hospice, I learned Roy passed away three weeks and a day after I was kicked out of our house. His daughters ended up having to sneak him out of the house to take him north over one hundred miles to Mel's home. His death was two days later. The trip had been too much. I gave my thanks it was finally over for him. I knew we would be together again in another world, wherever it might be.

His services were given by his son-in-law in Gaylord, and his remains cremated and placed next to his first wife, Mary's, in their home town of Taylor, Michigan.

Don't make the mistake in your online traveling I did when I began my trip. Unconsciously I was looking for another Ed. Remember, Dude taught me this. It isn't the "looks" but rather what the man is. Most men online are widowed, not divorced. Without realizing it they are looking for a woman like their departed wife.

In appearance, my Roy was nothing like my big handsome Ed. No, Roy was no taller than I. His good looks were not those of Ed. It was somewhere within him I found all those things I loved. I was not another Sally for him as she, his wife, was average height and a curly blond. I am tall and have long almost-straight hair, now in its gray stage.

Above all the "I dos and don'ts," be honest. Be absolutely honest about health problems, age, money—is it needed or to be shared? Roy and I methodically charted all our monthly financial obligations. With those two lists, we divided the total we would have living together. Those that were strictly ours such as life insurance remained ours to pay. Everything else, such as food, TV, rent, etc., was divided equally. As a result, we both ended up with more of our income to enjoy than we had when living alone. Our relationship brought *no* disappointment, only wonderful joy.

When an online man makes a silent decision without sharing it, don't do as I did with Clayton and Vic. I should have spoken up and asked them to listen to my thoughts on the problem. Do so gently, never with anger.

If their health is the reason for them to back away as it was for Clayton and Vic because they had come to love me so much they couldn't think of inflicting a sick man in my life, it is time to talk to them. Explain women by their very nature want to care for the one they love if illness descends. It is an important way they express their love. Just think how many women are nurses in our country. Remember my deep desire to become a physician? I performed this love for both my Ed and Roy.

Don't allow others like Roy's daughters prevent a marriage. Society will be slow in changing its rules about how we women must live. Hospice shared with me they had troubles with the families of their patients, not with the patients themselves. But do what is best and smile even if 105!

I intend to.

Finally, if the miles between are preventive, they can be erased. The many winter trips I drove back and forth to be with Roy accumulated to the distance which separate Vic and me.

31

Dead-End Road

My children and grandchildren arrived and shared their hugs, kisses, and gifts five weeks ago yesterday. It was March 1, my ninety-second birthday.

What a time we had! My granddaughters Melissa and Rachael arrived with yummy birthday cakes. And there were undreamed of gifts, including beautiful new drapes for my front sliding windows. Melissa's cake was a beautiful version of the traditional round-layered version with a heavily decorated icing. Rachael, who is only about six months older than her cousin, brought a large flat cake with unbelievable flavor—a very contemporary one. We enjoyed Melissa's celebration in the small restaurant in Charlevoix in which she is the cook. Rachael carried hers into my apartment on their arrival the next day from their home down near Grand Rapids. I can still feel the hug she gave me after setting the cake down on my table. "Oh, Grandma, I can't believe you are ninety-two!"

"Maybe I'm not," I replied. It was as if the sun had suddenly burst out within the small room.

Thanks to Doctor Jim's depressant pills Grace had helped me obtain, I had pretty well recovered from the horrible shock of Roy's unbelievable disappearance and unannounced death some three weeks later. My recovery had only been physically, that is. Deep inside, my head I was not certain I'd ever emotionally recover from his departure. Tears were always waiting to roll down my cheeks. They were hanging there even then. Grace, retired nurse professional that she was, had insisted I seek help from my Dr. Jim.

I held no anger toward Roy's two daughters. I believe it was what Roy's daughters observed and heard from others which controlled their thoughts. Back when I first met the younger daughter three years before, she laughingly told me about the time she had tried so hard to get Roy to go online to look for a woman during the year following his Mary's death. Yes, it had been her idea back then, not his.

When 2015 emerged on all our calendars, some five months after Roy's unreported death, I found myself once again becoming interested in my computer's daily "knocks."

Oh, this had nothing to do with my decision to man hunt again, but rather for the opportunity to have an online friend I would enjoy in my lonely life. I understood I was way too old to be of any true interest to any man, no matter his age. After all, I had discovered my brother had been correct. They were all seven-second thinkers and didn't understand what it is we women enjoy and want even in our nineties. Or that special love is our need and dream also. We have been convinced women aren't to mention it, and so we don't.

Not a single one grasped the idea an "old" woman may be just as hungry for a seven-second time with a man as he does. No, society has convinced men and even many women that they hold no ability to share their love with a man once they reach their fifties and sixties, let alone their nineties.

For years I had had a loving husband, raised two families of children, and busily did things for others and my community. The year 2015 found all this missing in my life. On top of it all was Roy's disappearance. To be alone in a small apartment in the heart of a cold winter had never been the way of life for me.

I could no longer bundle up and get over to Boyne Mountain to ski. Those days were past. About once a week, I would bake an apple pie and join Susie and Pat for dinner on their beautifully snow-covered farm. Their friendship and laughter were the best medicine available, much more effective than the doctor's depressant pills. Their home way out in the country next to the head waters of the Jordan River was the essence of hominess. I always felt "at home" when with those two. It was heaven to be with them.

The research interest I still harbored soon discovered online dating had changed in the three years I had been away. I couldn't believe the number of local- and state-wide correspondents who had joined the game. This was great as it indicated older persons tapping online would have a much better opportunity to be closer to each other when on their monitor windows. Much less mileage lay between them than had between me, Clayton, Vic, or Will.

But I did find myself writing to some to compliment them on their venture and encourage them to not give up and to be honest with those they wrote. I never suggested they might find me interesting. After all, I had found my man even though he had been stolen from me. I had been successful in my search and would always have the memories of the time we had with other and the places we journeyed.

The week following my ninety-second birthday found me plunged back into the deep pit of discouragement which had surrounded me following Clayton's, Will's, Vic's, and Roy's departures. My joyous birthday celebrations with my family backed away as the new days arrived and then left. Monday through Friday, I found myself completely shot. I was staring at my walls all by myself. No one knocked on my door or called on the phone. I kept myself awake by playing endless games of my version of solitaire. Yes, there was music from the TV—Roy and my favorite country music. He sat across the room from me on the comfy flower-covered couch we had bought. No matter when I glanced his way, he was there smiling at me.

My family was far away busy with their own great lives. Their love was left with me, I knew, yet they themselves weren't near. I was determined not to do anything to disrupt them.

Oh, I had wonderful neighbors. Christy, the older woman across the parking lot from me, had managed to get out and clean the snow from my car all winter before I was even out of bed. She used her broom. A high school freshman, Stacy frequently came over to use my computer during the evenings. His family had none. His sister, a fifth grader, was one of my little four-member once-a-week after-school art class I held every Thursday afternoon.

Jason, a thirty-year-old, and Mary, his wife-to-be, were like grandchildren to me. He had health concerns, which I tried to help him manage, and he was constantly on call to help me with computer problems. He had tried to link me with his beloved grandfather but again the thirty some miles between us were impenetrable as he no longer drove. And there was Jim, my computer doctor. When it had problems beyond Jason's abilities, Jim came to the apartment to do its repairs. We had such a great time. He was always successful.

Despite all this, my life had become meaningless and lonely. No matter where I glanced in my cozy apartment's living room—home of my office, TV, books, and paintings could I find anyone to talk to or do for. Every object my eyes lit upon only brought back memories of days long gone when my life was so wonderfully busy.

My mind roamed, remembered the past, the places I had been and the people I was with. So it was a week after my birthday on Sunday evening as I sat in my comfy blue living-room chair I decided the time had arrived for me to move down to Grand Rapids to a rest home. Near my beloved granddaughter Rachael, I would wait out the final days of my life. I would endeavor not to become her responsibility. Maybe I could teach an art class or find some writing I could do. Grand Rapids was a good-sized city and had a very active art group. Hopefully I could find more to do than sit by the hour playing solitaire. My cards had become my companion throughout my long days since Roy left.

I pulled myself out of my comfy chair and picked my phone up off my desk and headed back to my chair. Once I had settled myself back in it, my little cell phone suddenly rang. No, it wasn't Rachael but William Pellett, one of the online men I was enjoying corresponding with.

He had impressed me, but I had convinced myself I was too old to be considering a replacement of Roy. William was only eighty-nine.

"Hello, Anne. This is William Pellett. I haven't heard from you these last three days and am wondering if everything is okay with you?"

His voice had a thickness to it. He sounded so masculine. And yet underneath all that, I sensed laughter, a smile and happiness.

"Hi there, William. No, I'm okay. Just having a hard time being alone after all the great fun I had last weekend with my family. Remember, they were here celebrating my birthday with me. I miss them so darn much. They all live far, far away—even those here in Michigan. It's better than it used to be I have to admit 'cause Rachael and her Rutt just moved back here from Washington, DC, last summer."

"That's one of the major reasons I believe you would be happy here with me," William answered. "All seven of my children live nearby. Betty and Earl even live 'next door' on my farm. Betty's son and his family live here also. Every Sunday I have my door open to all my family for those who can come for a noon get-together and lunch. I have had as many as thirty-five show up. Oh, I so wish you could be here with all of us. I know you would be happier than where you are now."

"Boy, do you sound happy, William. I envy you."

"I love them all, Anne. Yet once they leave, I am all alone. I have never been alone in my long life, and it is more than I can take. As I told you, my Sally died last June after ten years with a stroke. I am so used to her at my side and our love. This way of living isn't for me. Won't you consider coming over and letting me be part of your life and you part of mine? I think we would find the love we both need."

He continued, "My home and family would all be yours. Anne, I have problems with my feet and diabetes. But Betty would drive me over to meet you if you feel the drive over here is too much. I so want you to see my home and meet my kids. I need you here with me night and day."

There I sat listening to a man tell me of his need for me. I knew everything he said was true. I had all those same feelings. Yet they had not included him. No, I had convinced myself such a life could no longer be mine. I was too old. Obviously my age wasn't part of William's thinking. He saw me as the answer he desired.

I asked myself, "What is this that is going on here in my living room right at the moment I had decided my life was over?"

"You have no idea, William, what your words are doing to me. I hardly know you, and yet I feel as if we have known each other for years. We have had lives so different, and yet we think the same about what is ours and what we want even now. For me, as you said, life without love is impossible. Why not meet and see if we are each other's answer for the days ahead. I am not going to ask you to have your daughter make the trip over here with you. No, I love to drive and am good at it. I will get myself in my bedroom and pack my suitcase. Tomorrow morning I will leave Boyne City for Menomonie, Wisconsin, at 9:00 a.m. Give me my directions, please."

"Anne! I can't believe what you just said. Oh, my darling woman, I am so excited."

He then proceeded to tell me how to locate him on 750th Ave. just northwest of Menomonie, Wisconsin. His home was on his four-hundred-acre dairy farm and the shore of Tainter Lake. Although retired, he still was in his farmhouse home.

William had been talking to me for well over an hour. After our good-byes, I laid my phone down, walked into my bed room to pull my suitcase out of its closet. William's obvious need of me in his life had brought back my world to me. Once again, I was aware of my need for another and his love. And as always, there were miles between us—over five hundred. But my online traveling had taught me if I wanted someone, I very well might be the one who would have to do the journeying. I had been the one who flew to Clayton and Vic, drove to Ray, and found Will by using a train. No man had driven to be with me, not even Mr. Malaysia, although he had offered. Yet William was different. His reason that he not be the traveler was based on a health issue—his feet.

I had nodded my head yes as I listened to William. As we hung up, I told him, "William, I will see you tomorrow evening. I am going to pack my bag and prepare myself to be on my way tomorrow morning about nine,"

"Oh, my darling woman, I can't believe you will be in my arms tomorrow. I will have dinner ready."

I laid down my phone and walked into my bedroom to pull a suitcase out of my closet. Paul had asked me to marry him. The over five hundred miles separating us was of no concern to him. He had offered two suggested solutions to erase the miles. The choice had been placed in my lap.

He lived on his dairy farm about two miles north of Menomonie, Wisconsin. I wasn't certain the distance involved but it made no difference in his thinking. Fortunately I loved to drive, so it was not a barrier to me as it probably would have been to many others. His logical words and voice caused me to feel as if I was wrapped in his arms. They were there to love me the rest of my days. I knew we had to meet.

After methodically packing, I dragged my suitcase out to the apartment's front door. This was all a result of William's call—of his logical persuasion. I was going to drive to Wisconsin to meet him. He had convinced me we should stand face to face. He would drive to Michigan to meet me but hoped I would come to him. He felt it important I see his home. It would become mine if we discovered in each other the person we longed so for. It all made sense. His reasoning made sense. My experience online told me to do what I could to have this happen. My love of driving made it all sound exciting. I would have something worthwhile to do when I crawled out of bed the following day—a Monday morning. The weather prediction was for sunshine and a springlike day.

Unlike my other four proposals, William was including me in making our decision. Just the fact he was doing so convinced me he was the kind of man I yearned to be with.

I knew full heartedly what I planned to do was absolutely insane for an ancient ninety-two-year-old woman to embark on by herself in today's world thinking habits. However for me and my situation, it wasn't. Yet in the thinking of anyone who heard of my venture, it would seem so. The wonderful cash birthday gift my son had given me would buy the gas the trip would require. I would tell no one, not even Grace. After all, the roads I would use wouldn't be heavy with traffic. There would be no large cities to drive through. No, most of the journey would be with beautiful Lake Michigan, rolling hills and forests outside my car's windows.

With my courage seated beside me, I'd head northwest over the Mackinac Bridge and across the southern edge of Michigan's Upper Peninsula into Wisconsin. I had driven almost forty miles day after day to meet Roy, so why not William? Yes, I would head northwestward to meet William Pellett. His gleaming eyes, intelligent words, and wonderful online smile were telling me to come to him.

In his phone call, William had convinced me my age bothered him not at all. It had nothing to do with love, which is a given gift to be shared. He was an eighty-nine-year-old retired dairy farmer with seven children, most lived nearby. His farmhouse sat on the edge of Tainter Lake about two miles north of Menomonie. He would have dinner ready for me.

In our online visits, we had learned we had lived overflowing lives, were involved in WWII, attended college, had wonderful marriages, great families, travels, done things for others, treasured our churches, and clasped strong beliefs in the Lord. We had both nursed our beloved mates for more than eight years before their deaths. Our love for them had never ended. It was because of all this we were so desperately lonely and needed each other.

Suddenly, what I had learned during the time I was with Clayton, Vic, Will, and others returned to my mind. This time, I would not let the man's decisions dissolve my opportunity to have a love. No, I would be the one to make the miles disappear. Nothing would prevent me from having the opportunity to meet and know this man. Although to me William's house and nearby family weren't major issues, I respected his viewpoint. I would make the trip. If I found only disappointment, I would stay in a motel and return to my apartment the following day. Once back, I'd head for Grand Rapids to be near my Rachael.

The following day, I left without telling anyone what I was up to. I didn't want to cause anyone worrying. I knew they would. It was a gorgeous sunny day, and the trip a straight arrow which shot across Michigan UP's route 2 and on to Wisconsin's 64. I had driven the Michigan roads many times on camping trips—wonderful memories returned as I moved westward.

Back in '57 in an effort to convince my Ed we as a family should be taking summer vacations, I had packed our hunky German Shepherd and the four kids into our big Mercury station wagon along with all my parents' camping gear and left our Maumee, Ohio, country *McCall's* home for Michigan's Upper Peninsula. Contrary to his and my brother, David's opposition we had a wonderful week. We even made it all the way west to stay in Porcupine State Park. Oh, yes, memories were everywhere.

As the miles flew behind me, I sat behind my steering wheel silently laughing over the old bag driving five hundred miles to check out a man. Then I prayed by doing so, others would be encouraged to reach out in their search for a life companion in their late years. Yes, it was exciting and challenging. The roads were all in great shape and easy to follow. Along the way I saw signs of huge lumbering operations and trains waiting to be filled with logs piled beside the tracks. In other areas, the farms looked so prosperous and the small towns happy places. Rivers and deep forests shared their beauty and seclusion beneath the sunny blue ski. Somewhere deep within me, I was certain William would be the man my whole search had been about. My world glistened.

Late in the evening, probably about ten o'clock at the very end of my trip, I found myself lost all because of the Dead-End Road sign above the entry of the road back to his home. William had not mentioned it. Somehow it said I wasn't where I should be. Looking back I think I must have been tired from the long trip but completely unaware of my feelings. No, I was too excited. I backed out and drove the two miles on into Menominee.

As it was approaching eleven o'clock businesses were closed, even gas stations. I decided to call Paul and get the directions I needed.

His answer was, "Stay right where you are and I will come bring you back to the house."

I had driven off and parked on a little side road right where it hooked onto the main highway. There was no traffic. It was pretty late by then. A few minutes later, I saw a car coming my way. As it approached, I waved out my car window to flag it down.

The driver waved back, turned in beside my car, then moved back into the highway, drove to its opposite side, and stopped, waiting for me.

I hadn't been able to see the driver in the night's darkness but was certain it was William. He had stopped to be sure I was the Anne he wanted to "pick up." I understood and did the same, pulling up behind him so I could walk up to his window and check out his identity.

Just as I was crawling out of my car (I am slow moving up and out), he drove off.

I reached for my cell phone to call and ask him to slow down until I caught up. Much to my horror, my phone was dead! During the whole process of preparing my trip and then jumping in the car, I had completely forgotten its need for charges. I knew I had to locate a usable phone fast as William had disappeared out of site over a hill.

I was ticked. Why couldn't he have been more patient? I suspected he probably was pretty ticked about such a stupid woman. I turned around and headed on into town. I could tell I was close to its center. It was my hope I could locate a telephone to call William just down the road somewhere as it was approaching eleven o'clock. Businesses were closed, even gas stations.

My luck stayed with me as I spotted one which still had interior lighting. A young man could be seen working at his desk through one of the windows. I rapped on it, and he came to my aid.

"I'm from Michigan here to visit a friend but I can't find their house and my cell phone is dead. Could I please use yours?" He grinned and nodded yes.

Using his phone, I reached William who had returned to his home only two miles away as there was no way for him to locate me. He had been the one I had flagged down. He had recognized me and driven over to park until I could get out in the road to be behind him. He had taken off thinking I would be following him back to his home.

When I had turned around instead, he didn't know where to look, so he had given me up and gone on home. He figured I would call again, and he didn't have his phone with him. I had left him no choice.

All together, it took us over an hour to discover each other, but we succeeded. He drove to the station and spotted me leaning against my little Focus. His car pulled up right next to where I stood. He jumped out, arms wide open, and his wonderful grin aimed at me. They were screaming "I love you." In his arms, I felt his welcome. Not once did he question me or scold me for the stupid things I had done. No, it was obvious the gas station was not where he wanted us to be together. He wanted me home with him. We took off. I followed him as he led me back to his home. Yes, it was at the end of the dead-end road! I had been right where I had wanted to be!

To this day, he has not scolded me about it all—no, he laughs whenever our memories take us back to the night on March 9, 2015, when I was ninety-two and he, eighty-nine.

32

Atlasta Farm

Yes, at the very end of a narrow, curvy road through a woods, William's home waited for us. A one-story white house with red trim it was tucked back in the woods, but the ground beneath the tall pines and maples was mowed. It was his yard. He had left his garage door open, and the front porch lights were glistening. But what I saw wasn't what really was sitting before me. No, Will's home is two-storied with its full exterior only exposed across its backside, which is fifteen feet from Tainter Lake shore glistening below it about ten feet.

Once he swung the door open, I could see supper waiting. The clock above the table told me it was eleven thirty in Wisconsin not twelve thirty as it was back in Boyne. My joy over making it to Will's and his in having me with him generated chatter and laughter. We shook our heads over my long drive all by myself and then the stupid mess I created by getting lost at the trip's end. We laughed ourselves crazy over it all. Then it was back to the end of the hall to his bedroom on the western end of the house. So it was to bed to better say hello and discover the love we both so cherished. Immediately, we understood it was to be ours until the ends of our lives. Neither of us could believe the wonderful life we had discovered. We both understood it could never have happened without today's cyberspace world—absolutely not.

Will affected me just as my Ed had the night I had first seen him standing at the base of the dorm's stairs on the OSU campus. My whole body responded. My first glimpse of Will moving toward me with his arms outstretched at the Menomonie gas station had produced the same awesome reaction.

Without our online visiting, I would have been sitting in a lonely retirement home near Rachael waiting to die. To this very day, I can't explain, nor can Will, how we were so fortunate as to be together. There is nothing strange about Will to me at all. It is as if both of us have known each other our entire lives. We talk of his Sally and my Ed and both our families as well as where we've been and what we have done as if it is important to catch up on ourselves with each other.

He has memories of his service in WWII as I have about the same time with my Ed. His college years were concentrated into only three years while I took the traditional four to receive my degree. His was in the field of agriculture. He had grown up on his father's farm and been his dad's helper. In the end, he had returned to farming on his own four-hundred-acre dairy farm. The house we live in is the home he built on the edge of the farm which backs up to Tainter Lake. The beautiful lake was created when the local electric company built a large dam across Tainter River to produce its power. The Tainter name is that of the prominent lumberman who lived in this region back in the lumber days.

Being the outdoor lover I am living here with Will is an unbelievable miracle. The farm is all composed of hills and valleys on the lake's shore. Today, his eldest son Earl, who lives next door, owns the farm. He has a large herd of huge black bulls, which graze across the street from our house down the road a bit. I am in awe of them and their sizes. A daughter and her family and his grandson and also live down the road a bit.

Every Sunday, family members come to our home to join us for dinner about one o'clock. Will's church and now mine convenes at 9:30 a.m., so we are home in plenty of time to prepare the food. To top this off, most of those who arrive bring something to share on the table. All summer days William's son, John cooks the meat on the outdoor grill. The grandchildren love their grandfather's huge supply of ice cream goodies. Unfortunately, I do too. The church is about five miles farther into the country than we are. The farms here are enormous, stretching for miles across the valleys and even up and over the hills. The corn this year is taller and more beautiful than Will can remember ever having observed before. I love to have him tell me stories of former years when he operated his farm. I am learning a lot.

The day following my arrival, Will drove us into Menomonie, just two miles down the main road to go shopping. Yes, he took me into a jewelry store, and together, we found my engagement-wedding ring. We made plans to have my son-in-law Paul perform the ceremony back in Cadillac, Michigan.

That was the last time he drove the car as I took it over from then on. It was very noticeable as his foot due to his diabetes would every so often fall off the gas pedal. The result was a jerky ride. I am so thankful to be able to do the driving for him. Well, I actually drive, but he sits to my right and tells me exactly where to turn, what lane I should be in, etc. It is wonderful as Wisconsin's country cross roads are engineered differently than those in Michigan. There are no simple cross roads. I appreciate his words of wisdom.

Now, a few weeks later, I am sharing this happy ending with you in my new office (a former first floor bedroom) which overlooks Tainter Lake. Two weeks after my arrival at William's home, he chose to return to Michigan with me. There we packed my belongings and brought those I needed back to our home in Wisconsin thanks to Jim Cook's help. Most of my furniture in the apartment as well as all the kitchen equipment and other things in other closets and cupboards were tucked away in a storage garage in Boyne. Down the road, the three grandchildren we raised plan to purchase a vacation home there. It is where they grew up and is "home" to them. Its ski hills and lake will make a wonderful retreat center in which they can spend time together with their children down the road. When that happens, everything in the garage will be theirs to use within their new home. It thrills me Pat, Rachael, and Laura remain so caring and close to each other. Once I leave this earth, they will have no parent beside them.

Once Will and I returned back home, I discovered his two nearby daughters had completely emptied the main floor bedroom I wanted to use as my office and sewing room. There I hung the large photos of my family members and other memorabilia, lined my books up on the big shelves I moved over with me, and set my desk and sewing table plus my file cabinets in usable locations. I was at home.

The very following week, we once again climbed into his red Buick and turned west. William had tried to visit the Grand Canyon some twenty years before with his Sally. When they were almost there, she had tripped over a small rock and fallen trying to take a photo of him. The bang ups were too serious for them to make it into the canyon.

With me behind, the steering wheel he envisioned himself finishing that long before try. As I had stood on the canyon's edge briefly back in December '45 beside my Ed on our way home from the war, it was a completion of my time also. The trip beside Will through our unbelievable country was a honeymoon I couldn't believe. Even his four-day hospital stay in Flagstaff didn't interfere as I stayed in the room with him. There was a large chair which converted into a bed for me. No, for that short time, we didn't share a bed. There were way too many electronic gadgets attached to my Will. The doctors knew exactly what to do for a person whose heart had reacted to the town's high elevation. And William knew carrying a portable oxygen dispenser with him would allow us to reach the Canyon's edge. Yes, we made it—all 2,500 miles!

I have shared this "happy ending" with my family and William with his. His friends look at him, then me, and happy grins glow on their faces. We have traveled back to Michigan via the Lake Michigan ferry to camp with my grandchildren at the Ludington State park, and then northward to have my entire family meet Will and to say hello to friends in Boyne City. This included Grace, Susie, and Pat, as well as my pastor, Beth. On the way back to Wisconsin, we met with my David at Mackinaw City.

During our stop in Cadillac, my son-in-law, Pastor Paul Tomlinson, performed our church blessing marriage for us before the altar in his wonderful old church. It thrilled me to see the contentment and happiness every family member and friend experienced on being with Will and knowing the unbelievable happiness we share now and will forever more. Our happiness is so obvious.

How did this all happen and why? Because the Lord created in us love, which we can give to each other to enjoy and share every minute of our days and nights. The world needs to welcome this love which can surround each of us.

I must share an awesome fact as I leave. It will bring laughter, big time! My Ed had an old Aunt Hattie who was a physician in lower Illinois in the early 1900s. Yes, she succeeded in entering a man's profession, the one I so wanted to embrace even later in the game. She lived on a farm she called Atlasta Farm. Ed and I visited it way back in 1945 on our way home at the war's closing.

Twenty-five years later, Ed bought a cherry orchard-dairy farm one mile outside and north of Boyne City for us to call home. He named it Atlasta Farm in memory of his aunt's. In 1983 when I started my little quilting business, I named my small Michigan corporation Atlasta Farm.

The morning after my arrival on William's huge four-hundred-acre farm, he walked me about to show me its features. Back of his home stands a huge old white barn. On the end facing us was his farm's name, Atlasta Farm. I knew right then for the balance of my wonderful life I would indeed be at home with the unbelievable man who stood beside me, his arm about me and love in his eyes.

I am so thankful I had erased the over five hundred miles which spread itself out between Will and me. I had learned this was necessary during my traveling in cyberspace. Oh, yes, there is always a seemingly insurmountable wall. But I now know such walls are imaginary!